"THEY SAY / I SAY"

The Moves That Matter

in Academic Writing

Second Edition

"THEY SAY / I SAY"

The Moves That Matter

in Academic Writing

Second Edition

GERALD GRAFF

CATHY BIRKENSTEIN

both of the University of Illinois at Chicago

W · W · NORTON & COMPANY

NEW YORK   LONDON

For
Aaron David

W. W. Norton & Company has been independent since its founding in 1923, when William Warder Norton and Mary D. Herter Norton first published lectures delivered at the People's Institute, the adult education division of New York City's Cooper Union. The Nortons soon expanded their program beyond the Institute, publishing books by celebrated academics from America and abroad. By mid-century, the two major pillars of Norton's publishing program—trade books and college texts—were firmly established. In the 1950s, the Norton family transferred control of the company to its employees, and today—with a staff of four hundred and a comparable number of trade, college, and professional titles published each year—W. W. Norton & Company stands as the largest and oldest publishing house owned wholly by its employees.

Composition by Matrix Publishing Services, Inc.
Book design by Maggie Wagner
Production manager: Jane Searle

Library of Congress Cataloging-in-Publication Data

Graff, Gerald.
    They say / I say : the moves that matter in academic writing / Gerald Graff, Cathy Birkenstein.—2nd ed.
        p. cm.
    Includes bibliographical references and index.
    ISBN 978-0-393-93361-1 (pbk.)
    1. English language—Rhetoric—Handbooks, manuals, etc. 2. Persuasion (Rhetoric)—Handbooks, manuals, etc. 3. Report writing—Handbooks, manuals, etc. I. Birkenstein, Cathy. II. Title.
    PE1431.G73 2010
    808'.042—dc22
                                                          2009047993

W. W. Norton & Company, Inc., 500 Fifth Avenue, New York, N.Y. 10110
                        www.wwnorton.com

W. W. Norton & Company Ltd., Castle House, 75/76 Wells Street,
London W1T 3QT

    3 4 5 6 7 8 9 0

Brief Contents

—◻—

CONTENTS

Contents

Preface
to the Second Edition

—◻—

AT THE CORE OF THIS BOOK is the premise that good argumentative writing begins not with an act of assertion but an act of listening, of putting ourselves in the shoes of those who think differently from us. As a result, we advise writers to begin not with what they themselves think about their subject ("I say") but with what others think ("they say"). This practice, we think, adds urgency to writing, helping it become more authentically motivated. When writing responds to something that has been said or might be said, it thereby performs the meaningful task of supporting, correcting, or complicating that other view.

As we have traveled the country to some of the thousand plus colleges and universities where *They Say / I Say* is being used, we have been inspired by the many instructors and students who have praised our work, challenged it, and taken our ideas in new and unexpected directions. We have tried hard to take our own advice and to listen closely to what those using this book have said and asked for—and to respond as best we can in this new edition.

One thing that has been particularly heartening to see is the wide variety of disciplinary applications to which this book has been put. Though we originally intended it for use in first-year writing courses, we are delighted to find that it is being taught in many other courses and disciplines across the curriculum:

college success courses and first-year seminars; history, biology, political science, sociology—and more. But while teachers in these fields have been highly resourceful in adapting our methods to the special conventions of their disciplines, many of them have suggested we pay more attention in the book to how the core moves of entering conversations operate in fields and courses beyond our own.

Accordingly, this edition contains **two new chapters,** one by biologist Christopher Gillen on **Writing in the Sciences,** the other by political scientist Erin Ackerman on **Writing in the Social Sciences.** To show that writing in those fields is fundamentally argumentative and not, as some imagine, exclusively factual or informational, these chapters adapt our templates to help students with the specific demands of writing in those fields. And to demonstrate further how the rhetorical moves taught in this book work across domains and disciplines, we've added readings at the back of the book by a journalist, a humanist, a physicist, and a linguist.

Also new to this edition is a **chapter on reading,** an earlier version of which was first published in *"They Say / I Say" with Readings.* This chapter grew out of our own experience teaching with the first edition, where we found that the writing templates in this book had the unexpected benefit of improving reading comprehension. We found, in addition, that when students worked with a template like "many people believe _____, but my own view is _____," it helped them see how the authors they were reading were part of a conversation that the students themselves could enter—and thus to see reading as a matter not of passively absorbing information but of understanding and actively entering dialogues and debates.

We've tried to make the book even **easier to use,** with cross-references in the margins, leading students to specific examples, instructions, and more detail where they might need it.

Several other new features of this edition are worth mentioning. One is an expanded discussion of the controversial question of the first person "I," pointing out that academic writers across most disciplines now tend to make liberal use of "I," "we," and their variants. Finally, responding to students' frequent questions about plagiarism, we've explained why using generic phrases like "on the one hand . . . on the other hand" does not constitute academic dishonesty.

Even as we have revised and added to *"They Say / I Say,"* our basic goals remain unchanged: to demystify academic writing and reading by identifying the key moves of persuasive argument and representing these moves in forms that students can put into practice.

PREFACE

Demystifying Academic Conversation

——⬚——

EXPERIENCED WRITING INSTRUCTORS have long recognized that writing well means entering into conversation with others. Academic writing in particular calls upon writers not simply to express their own ideas, but to do so as a response to what others have said. The first-year writing program at our own university, according to its mission statement, asks "students to participate in ongoing conversations about vitally important academic and public issues." A similar statement by another program holds that "intellectual writing is almost always composed in response to others' texts." These statements echo the ideas of rhetorical theorists like Kenneth Burke, Mikhail Bakhtin, and Wayne Booth as well as recent composition scholars like David Bartholomae, John Bean, Patricia Bizzell, Irene Clark, Greg Colomb, Lisa Ede, Peter Elbow, Joseph Harris, Andrea Lunsford, Elaine Maimon, Gary Olson, Mike Rose, John Swales and Christine Feak, Tilly Warnock, and others who argue that writing well means engaging the voices of others and letting them in turn engage us.

Yet despite this growing consensus that writing is a social, conversational act, helping student writers actually participate in these conversations remains a formidable challenge. This book aims to meet that challenge. Its goal is to demystify academic writing by isolating its basic moves, explaining them clearly, and representing them in the form of templates. In this way, we hope to help students become active participants in the important conversations of the academic world and the wider public sphere.

HIGHLIGHTS

- *Shows students that writing well means entering a conversation,* summarizing others ("they say") to set up one's own argument ("I say").
- *Demystifies academic writing,* showing students "the moves that matter" in language they can readily apply.
- *Provides user-friendly templates* to help writers make those moves in their own writing.

HOW THIS BOOK CAME TO BE

The original idea for this book grew out of our shared interest in democratizing academic culture. First, it grew out of arguments that Gerald Graff has been making throughout his career that schools and colleges need to invite students into the conversations and debates that surround them. More specifically, it is a practical, hands-on companion to his recent book, *Clueless in Academe: How Schooling Obscures the Life of the Mind,* in which he looks at academic conversations from the perspective of those who find them mysterious and proposes ways in which such mystification can be overcome. Second, this book grew out of writing templates that Cathy Birkenstein developed in the 1990s, for use in writing and literature courses she was teaching. Many students, she found, could readily grasp what it meant to support a thesis with evidence, to entertain a counterargument, to identify a textual contradiction, and ultimately to summarize and respond to challenging arguments, but they often had trouble putting these concepts into practice in their own writing. When Cathy sketched out templates on the board, however, giving her students some of the language and patterns that these sophisticated moves require, their writing—and even their quality of thought—significantly improved.

This book began, then, when we put our ideas together and realized that these templates might have the potential to open up and clarify academic conversation. We proceeded from the premise that all writers rely on certain stock formulas that they themselves didn't invent—and that many of these formulas are so commonly used that they can be represented in model templates that students can use to structure and even generate what they want to say.

As we developed a working draft of this book, we began using it in first-year writing courses that we teach at UIC. In classroom exercises and writing assignments, we found that students who otherwise struggled to organize their thoughts, or even to think of something to say, did much better when we provided them with templates like the following.

▸ In discussions of _____, a controversial issue is whether _____. While some argue that _____, others contend that _____.

▸ This is not to say that _____.

One virtue of such templates, we found, is that they focus writers' attention not just on what is being said, but on the *forms* that structure what is being said. In other words, they make students more conscious of the rhetorical patterns that are key to academic success but often pass under the classroom radar.

THE CENTRALITY OF "THEY SAY / I SAY"

The central rhetorical move that we focus on in this book is the "they say / I say" template that gives our book its title. In our view, this template represents the deep, underlying structure, the internal DNA as it were, of all effective argument. Effective persuasive writers do more than make well-supported claims ("I say"); they also map those claims relative to the claims of others ("they say").

Here, for example, the "they say / I say" pattern structures a passage from a recent essay by the media and technology critic Steven Johnson.

> For decades, we've worked under the assumption that mass culture follows a path declining steadily toward lowest-common-denominator standards, presumably because the "masses" want dumb, simple pleasures and big media companies try to give the masses what they want. But . . . the exact opposite is happening: the culture is getting more cognitively demanding, not less.
>
> STEVEN JOHNSON, *"Watching TV Makes You Smarter"*

In generating his own argument from something "they say," Johnson suggests *why* he needs to say what he is saying: to correct a popular misconception.

Even when writers do not explicitly identify the views they are responding to, as Johnson does, an implicit "they say" can often be discerned, as in the following passage by Zora Neale Hurston.

> I remember the day I became colored.
>
> ZORA NEALE HURSTON, *"How It Feels to Be Colored Me"*

In order to grasp Hurston's point here, we need to be able to reconstruct the implicit view she is responding to and questioning: that racial identity is an innate quality we are simply born with. On the contrary, Hurston suggests, our race is imposed on us by society—something we "become" by virtue of how we are treated.

As these examples suggest, the "they say / I say" model can improve not just student writing, but student reading comprehension as well. Since reading and writing are deeply reciprocal activities, students who learn to make the rhetorical moves represented by the templates in this book figure to become more adept at identifying these same moves in the texts they read. And if we are right that effective arguments are always in dialogue with other arguments, then it follows that in order to understand the types of challenging texts assigned in college, students need to identify the views to which those texts are responding.

Working with the "they say / I say" model can also help with invention, finding something to say. In our experience, students best discover what they want to say not by thinking about a subject in an isolation booth, but by reading texts, listening closely to what other writers say, and looking for an opening through which they can enter the conversation. In other words, listening closely to others and summarizing what they have to say can help writers generate their own ideas.

THE USEFULNESS OF TEMPLATES

Our templates also have a generative quality, prompting students to make moves in their writing that they might not otherwise make or even know they should make. The templates in this book can be particularly helpful for students who are unsure about what to say, or who have trouble finding enough to say, often because they consider their own beliefs so self-evident that they need not be argued for. Students like this are often helped, we've found, when we give them a simple template like the following one for entertaining a counterargument (or planting a naysayer, as we call it in Chapter 6).

> ▸ Of course some might object that _____. Although I concede that _____, I still maintain that _____.

What this particular template helps students do is make the seemingly counterintuitive move of questioning their own beliefs, of looking at them from the perspective of those who disagree. In so doing, templates can bring out aspects of students' thoughts that, as they themselves sometimes remark, they didn't even realize were there.

Other templates in this book help students make a host of sophisticated moves that they might not otherwise make: summarizing what someone else says, framing a quotation in one's own words, indicating the view that the writer is responding to, marking the shift from a source's view to the writer's own view, offering evidence for that view, entertaining and answering counterarguments, and explaining what is at stake in the first place. In showing students how to make such moves, templates do more than organize students' ideas; they help bring those ideas into existence.

OKAY, BUT TEMPLATES?

We are aware, of course, that some instructors may have reservations about templates. Some, for instance, may object that such formulaic devices represent a return to prescriptive forms of instruction that encourage passive learning or lead students to put their writing on automatic pilot.

This is an understandable reaction, we think, to kinds of rote instruction that have indeed encouraged passivity and drained writing of its creativity and dynamic relation to the social world. The trouble is that many students will never learn on their own to make the key intellectual moves that our templates represent. While seasoned writers pick up these moves unconsciously through their reading, many students do not. Consequently, we believe, students need to see these moves represented in the explicit ways that the templates provide.

The aim of the templates, then, is not to stifle critical thinking but to be direct with students about the key rhetorical moves that it comprises. Since we encourage students to modify and adapt the templates to the particularities of the arguments they are making, using such prefabricated formulas as learning tools need not result in writing and thinking that are themselves formulaic. Admittedly, no teaching tool can guarantee that students will engage in hard, rigorous thought. Our templates do, however, provide concrete prompts that can stimulate and shape such thought: What do "they say" about my topic? What would a naysayer say about my argument? What is my evidence? Do I need to qualify my point? Who cares?

In fact, templates have a long and rich history. Public orators from ancient Greece and Rome through the European Renaissance studied rhetorical *topoi* or "commonplaces," model passages and formulas that represented the different strategies available to public speakers. In many respects, our templates echo this classical rhetorical tradition of imitating established models.

The journal *Nature* requires aspiring contributors to follow a guideline that is like a template on the opening page of their manuscript: "Two or three sentences explaining what the main result [of their study] reveals in direct comparison with what was thought to be the case previously, or how the main result adds to previous knowledge." In the field of education, a form designed by the education theorist Howard Gardner asks postdoctoral fellowship applicants to complete the following template: "Most scholars in the field believe _____. As a result of my study, _____." That these two examples are geared toward postdoctoral fellows and veteran researchers shows that it is not only struggling undergraduates who can use help making these key rhetorical moves, but experienced academics as well.

Templates have even been used in the teaching of personal narrative. The literary and educational theorist Jane Tompkins devised the following template to help student writers make the often difficult move from telling a story to explaining what it means: "X tells a story about _____ to make the point that _____. My own experience with _____ yields a point that is similar/different/both similar and different. What I take away from my own experience with _____ is _____. As a result, I conclude _____." We especially like this template because it suggests that "they say / I say" argument need not be mechanical, impersonal, or dry, and that telling a story and making an argument are more compatible activities than many think.

WHY IT'S OKAY TO USE "I"

But wait—doesn't the "I" part of *"they say / I say"* flagrantly encourage the use of the first-person pronoun? Aren't we aware that some teachers prohibit students from using "I" or "we," on the grounds that these pronouns encourage ill-considered, subjective opinions rather than objective and reasoned arguments? Yes, we are aware of this first-person prohibition, but we think it has serious flaws. First, expressing ill-considered, subjective opinions is not necessarily the worst sin beginning writers can commit; it might be a starting point from which they can move on to more reasoned, less self-indulgent perspectives. Second, prohibiting students from using "I" is simply not an effective way of curbing students' subjectivity, since one can offer poorly argued, ill-supported opinions just as easily without it. Third and most important, prohibiting the first person tends to hamper students' ability not only to take strong positions but to differentiate their own positions from those of others, as we point out in Chapter 5. To be sure, writers can resort to various circumlocutions—"it will here be argued," "the evidence suggests," "the truth is"—and these may be useful for avoiding a monotonous series of "I believe" sentences. But except for avoiding such monotony, we see no good reason why "I" should be set aside in persuasive writing. Rather than prohibit "I," then, we think a better tactic is to give students practice at using it well and learning its use, both by supporting their claims with evidence and by attending closely to alternative perspectives—to what "they" are saying.

HOW THIS BOOK IS ORGANIZED

Because of its centrality, we have allowed the "they say / I say" format to dictate the structure of this book. So while Part 1 addresses the art of listening to others, Part 2 addresses how to offer one's own response. Part 1 opens with a chapter on "Starting with What Others Are Saying" that explains why it is generally advisable to begin a text by citing others rather than plunging directly into one's own views. Subsequent chapters take up the arts of summarizing and quoting what these others have to say. Part 2 begins with a chapter on different ways of responding, followed by chapters on marking the shift between what "they say" and what "I say," on introducing and answering objections, and on answering the all-important questions "so what?" and "who cares?" Part 3 offers strategies for "Tying It All Together," beginning with a chapter on connection and coherence; followed by a chapter on formal and informal language, arguing that academic discourse is often perfectly compatible with the informal language that students use outside school; and concluding with a chapter on the art of metacommentary, showing students how to guide the way readers understand a text. Part 4 offers guidance for entering conversations in specific academic situations, with chapters on class discussions, reading, and writing in the sciences and social sciences. Finally, we provide four readings and an index of templates.

WHAT THIS BOOK DOESN'T DO

There are some things that this book does not try to do. We do not, for instance, cover logical principles of argument such as syllogisms, warrants, logical fallacies, or the differences between inductive and deductive reasoning. Although such concepts can be useful, we believe most of us learn the ins and outs of argumentative writing not by studying logical principles in the abstract, but by plunging into actual discussions and debates, trying out different patterns of response, and in this way getting a sense of what works to persuade different audiences and what doesn't. In our view, people learn more about arguing from hearing someone say, "You miss my point. What I'm saying is not _____, but _____," or "I agree with you that _____, and would even add that _____," than they do from studying the differences between inductive and deductive reasoning. Such formulas give students an immediate sense of what it feels like to enter a public conversation in a way that studying abstract warrants and logical fallacies does not.

ENGAGING WITH THE IDEAS OF OTHERS

One central goal of this book is to demystify academic writing by returning it to its social and conversational roots. Although writing may require some degree of quiet and solitude, the "they say / I say" model shows students that they can best develop their arguments not just by looking inward but by doing what they often do in a good conversation with friends and family— by listening carefully to what others are saying and engaging with other views.

This approach to writing therefore has an ethical dimension, since it asks writers not simply to keep proving and reasserting what they already believe but to stretch what they believe by putting it up against beliefs that differ, sometimes radically, from their own. In an increasingly diverse, global society, this ability to engage with the ideas of others is especially crucial to democratic citizenship.

Gerald Graff
Cathy Birkenstein

INTRODUCTION

Entering the Conversation

—◻—

THINK ABOUT AN ACTIVITY that you do particularly well: cooking, playing the piano, shooting a basketball, even something as basic as driving a car. If you reflect on this activity, you'll realize that once you mastered it you no longer had to give much conscious thought to the various moves that go into doing it. Performing this activity, in other words, depends on your having learned a series of complicated moves—moves that may seem mysterious or difficult to those who haven't yet learned them.

The same applies to writing. Often without consciously realizing it, accomplished writers routinely rely on a stock of established moves that are crucial for communicating sophisticated ideas. What makes writers masters of their trade is not only their ability to express interesting thoughts but their mastery of an inventory of basic moves that they probably picked up by reading a wide range of other accomplished writers. Less experienced writers, by contrast, are often unfamiliar with these basic moves and unsure how to make them in their own writing. This book is intended as a short, user-friendly guide to the basic moves of academic writing.

One of our key premises is that these basic moves are so common that they can be represented in *templates* that you can use right away to structure and even generate your own writing. Perhaps the most distinctive feature of this book is its presentation of many such templates, designed to help you successfully enter not only the world of academic thinking and writing, but also the wider worlds of civic discourse and work.

Instead of focusing solely on abstract principles of writing, then, this book offers model templates that help you put those principles directly into practice. Working with these templates can give you an immediate sense of how to engage in the kinds of critical thinking you are required to do at the college level and in the vocational and public spheres beyond.

Some of these templates represent simple but crucial moves like those used to summarize some widely held belief.

▸ Many Americans assume that _____ .

Others are more complicated.

▸ On the one hand, _____ . On the other hand, _____ .

▸ Author X contradicts herself. At the same time that she argues _____ , she also implies _____ .

▸ I agree that _____ .

▸ This is not to say that _____ .

It is true, of course, that critical thinking and writing go deeper than any set of linguistic formulas, requiring that you question assumptions, develop strong claims, offer supporting reasons and evidence, consider opposing arguments, and so on. But these deeper habits of thought cannot be put into practice unless you have a language for expressing them in clear, organized ways.

STATE YOUR OWN IDEAS AS A
RESPONSE TO OTHERS

The single most important template that we focus on in this book is the "they say _____; I say _____" formula that gives our book its title. If there is any one point that we hope you will take away from this book, it is the importance not only of expressing your ideas ("I say") but of presenting those ideas as a *response to some other person or group* ("they say"). For us, the underlying structure of effective academic writing—and of responsible public discourse—resides not just in stating our own ideas but in listening closely to others around us, summarizing their views in a way that they will recognize, and responding with our own ideas in kind. Broadly speaking, academic writing is argumentative writing, and we believe that to argue well you need to do more than assert your own position. You need to enter a conversation, using what others say (or might say) as a launching pad or sounding board for your own views. For this reason, one of the main pieces of advice in this book is to write the voices of others into your text.

In our view, then, the best academic writing has one underlying feature: it is deeply engaged in some way with other people's views. Too often, however, academic writing is taught as a process of saying "true" or "smart" things in a vacuum, as if it were possible to argue effectively without being in conversation *with* someone else. If you have been taught to write a traditional five-paragraph essay, for example, you have learned how to develop a thesis and support it with evidence. This is good advice as far as it goes, but it leaves out the important fact that in the real world we don't make arguments without being provoked. Instead, we make arguments because someone has said or done something (or perhaps *not* said or done something) and we need to respond: "I can't see why you like the Lakers so much"; "I agree: it was a great film"; "That argument is contradictory." If it weren't for other people and our need to challenge, agree with, or otherwise respond to them, there would be no reason to argue at all.

To make an impact as a writer, you need to do more than make statements that are logical, well supported, and consistent. You must also find a way of entering a conversation with others' views—with something "they say." If your own argument doesn't identify the "they say" that you're responding to, it probably won't make sense. As Figure 1 suggests, *what* you are saying may be clear to your audience, but *why* you are saying it won't be. For it is what others are saying and thinking that motivates our writing and gives it a reason for being. It follows, then, as Figure 2 suggests, that your own argument—the thesis or "I say" moment of your text—should always be a response to the arguments of others.

Many writers make explicit "they say / I say" moves in their writing. One famous example is Martin Luther King Jr.'s "Let-

FIGURE 1

4

FIGURE 2

ter from Birmingham Jail," which consists almost entirely of King's eloquent responses to a public statement by eight clergymen deploring the civil rights protests he was leading. The letter—which was written in 1963, while King was in prison for leading a demonstration against racial injustice in Birmingham—is structured almost entirely around a framework of summary and response, in which King summarizes and then answers their criticisms. In one typical passage, King writes as follows.

> You deplore the demonstrations taking place in Birmingham. But your statement, I am sorry to say, fails to express a similar concern for the conditions that brought about the demonstrations.
>
> MARTIN LUTHER KING JR., "Letter from Birmingham Jail"

King goes on to agree with his critics that "It is unfortunate that demonstrations are taking place in Birmingham," yet he hastens to add that "it is even more unfortunate that the city's white power structure left the Negro community with no alternative." King's letter is so thoroughly conversational, in fact, that it could be rewritten in the form of a dialogue or play.

> King's critics:
> King's response:
> Critics:
> Response:

Clearly, King would not have written his famous letter were it not for his critics, whose views he treats not as objections to his already-formed arguments but as the motivating source of those arguments, their central reason for being. He quotes not only what his critics have said ("Some have asked: 'Why didn't you give the new city administration time to act?' "), but also things they *might* have said ("One may well ask: 'How can you advocate breaking some laws and obeying others?' ")—all to set the stage for what he himself wants to say.

A similar "they say / I say" exchange opens an essay about American patriotism by the social critic Katha Pollitt, who uses her own daughter's comment to represent the national fervor of post-9/11 patriotism.

> My daughter, who goes to Stuyvesant High School only blocks from the former World Trade Center, thinks we should fly the American flag out our window. Definitely not, I say: The flag stands for jingoism and vengeance and war. She tells me I'm wrong—the flag means standing together and honoring the dead and saying no to terrorism. In a way we're both right. . . .
>
> KATHA POLLITT, "Put Out No Flags"

As Pollitt's example shows, the "they" you respond to in crafting an argument need not be a famous author or someone known to your audience. It can be a family member like Pollitt's daughter, or a friend or classmate who has made a provocative claim. It can even be something an individual or a group might say—or a side of yourself, something you once believed but no longer do, or something you partly believe but also doubt. The important thing is that the "they" (or "you" or "she") represent some wider group with which readers might identify—in Pollitt's case, those who patriotically believe in flying the flag. Pollitt's example also shows that responding to the views of others need not always involve unqualified opposition. By agreeing and disagreeing with her daughter, Pollitt enacts what we call the "yes and no" response, reconciling apparently incompatible views.

See Chapter 4 for more on agreeing, but with a difference.

While King and Pollitt both identify the views they are responding to, some authors do not explicitly state their views but instead allow the reader to infer them. See, for instance, if you can identify the implied or unnamed "they say" that the following claim is responding to.

> I like to think I have a certain advantage as a teacher of literature because when I was growing up I disliked and feared books.
>
> GERALD GRAFF, "Disliking Books at an Early Age"

In case you haven't figured it out already, the phantom "they say" here is the common belief that in order to be a good teacher of literature, one must have grown up liking and enjoying books.

As you can see from these examples, many writers use the "they say / I say" format to agree or disagree with others, to challenge standard ways of thinking, and thus to stir up controversy. This point may come as a shock to you if you have always had the impression that in order to succeed academically you need to play it safe and avoid controversy in your writing, making statements that nobody can possibly disagree with. Though this view of writing may appear logical, it is actually a recipe for flat, lifeless writing and for writing that fails to answer what we call the "so what?" and "who cares?" questions. "William Shakespeare wrote many famous plays and sonnets" may be a perfectly true statement, but precisely because nobody is likely to disagree with it, it goes without saying and thus would seem pointless if said.

WAYS OF RESPONDING

Just because much argumentative writing is driven by disagreement, it does not follow that *agreement* is ruled out. Although argumentation is often associated with conflict and opposition, the type of conversational "they say / I say" argument that we focus on in this book can be just as useful when you agree as when you disagree.

▶ She argues _____, and I agree because _____.

▶ Her argument that _____ is supported by new research showing that _____.

Nor do you always have to choose between either simply agreeing *or* disagreeing, since the "they say / I say" format also works to both agree and disagree at the same time, as Pollitt illustrates above.

▸ He claims that _____, and I have mixed feelings about it. On the one hand, I agree that _____. On the other hand, I still insist that _____.

This last option—agreeing and disagreeing simultaneously—is one we especially recommend, since it allows you to avoid a simple yes or no response and present a more complicated argument, while containing that complication within a clear "on the one hand / on the other hand" framework.

While the templates we offer in this book can be used to structure your writing at the sentence level, they can also be expanded as needed to almost any length, as the following elaborated "they say / I say" template demonstrates.

In recent discussions of _____, a controversial issue has been whether _____. On the one hand, some argue that _____. From this perspective, _____. On the other hand, however, others argue that _____. In the words of _____, one of this view's main proponents, "_____." According to this view, _____. In sum, then, the issue is whether _____ or _____.

My own view is that _____. Though I concede that _____, I still maintain that _____. For example, _____. Although some might object that _____, I would reply that _____. The issue is important because _____.

If you go back over this template, you will see that it helps you make a host of challenging moves (each of which is taken up in forthcoming chapters in this book). First, the template helps you open your text by identifying an issue in some ongoing conversation or debate ("In recent discussions of _____, a

9

controversial issue has been _____ "), and then to map some of the voices in this controversy (by using the "on the one hand / on the other hand" structure). The template also helps you introduce a quotation ("In the words of"), to explain the quotation in your own words ("According to this view"), and—in a new paragraph—to state your own argument ("My own view is that"), to qualify your argument ("Though I concede that"), and then to support your argument with evidence ("For example"). In addition, the template helps you make one of the most crucial moves in argumentative writing, what we call "planting a naysayer in your text," in which you summarize and then answer a likely objection to your own central claim ("Although it might be objected that _____, I reply _____ "). Finally, this template helps you shift between general, over-arching claims ("In sum, then") and smaller-scale, supporting claims ("For example").

Again, none of us is born knowing these moves, especially when it comes to academic writing. Hence the need for this book.

DO TEMPLATES STIFLE CREATIVITY?

If you are like some of our students, your initial response to templates may be skepticism. At first, many of our students complain that using templates will take away their originality and creativity and make them all sound the same. "They'll turn us into writing robots," one of our students insisted. Another agreed, adding, "Hey, I'm a jazz musician. And we don't play by set forms. We create our own." "I'm in college now," another student asserted; "this is third-grade-level stuff."

In our view, however, the templates in this book, far from being "third-grade-level stuff," represent the stock in trade of sophisticated thinking and writing, and they often require a great deal of practice and instruction to use successfully. As for the belief that pre-established forms undermine creativity, we think it rests on a very limited vision of what creativity is all about. In our view, the above template and the others in this book will actually help your writing become *more* original and creative, not less. After all, even the most creative forms of expression depend on established patterns and structures. Most songwriters, for instance, rely on a time-honored verse-chorus-verse pattern, and few people would call Shakespeare uncreative because he didn't invent the sonnet or the dramatic forms that he used to such dazzling effect. Even the most avant-garde, cutting-edge artists (like improvisational jazz musicians) need to master the basic forms that their work improvises on, departs from, and goes beyond, or else their work will come across as uneducated child's play. Ultimately, then, creativity and originality lie not in the avoidance of established forms but in the imaginative use of them.

Furthermore, these templates do not dictate the *content* of what you say, which can be as original as you can make it, but only suggest a way of formatting *how* you say it. In addition, once you begin to feel comfortable with the templates in this book, you will be able to improvise creatively on them to fit new situations and purposes and find others in your reading. In other words, the templates offered here are learning tools to get you started, not structures set in stone. Once you get used to using them, you can even dispense with them altogether, for the rhetorical moves they model will be at your fingertips in an unconscious, instinctive way.

But if you still need proof that writing templates do not stifle creativity, consider the following opening to an essay on the fast-food industry that we've included at the back of this book.

If ever there were a newspaper headline custom-made for Jay Leno's monologue, this was it. Kids taking on McDonald's this week, suing the company for making them fat. Isn't that like middle-aged men suing Porsche for making them get speeding tickets? Whatever happened to personal responsibility?

I tend to sympathize with these portly fast-food patrons, though. Maybe that's because I used to be one of them.

DAVID ZINCZENKO, "Don't Blame the Eater"

Although Zinczenko relies on a version of the "they say / I say" formula, his writing is anything but dry, robotic, or uncreative. While Zinczenko does not explicitly use the words "they say" and "I say," the template still gives the passage its underlying structure: "*They say* that kids suing fast-food companies for making them fat is a joke; but *I say* such lawsuits are justified."

BUT ISN'T THIS PLAGIARISM?

"But isn't this plagiarism?" at least one student each year will usually ask. "Well, is it?" we respond, turning the question around into one the entire class can profit from. "We are, after all, asking you to use language in your writing that isn't your own—language that you 'borrow' or, to put it less delicately, steal from other writers."

Often, a lively discussion ensues that raises important questions about authorial ownership and helps everyone better understand the frequently confusing line between plagiarism and the legitimate use of what others say and how they say it. Students are quick to see that no one person owns a conventional formula like "on the one hand . . . on the other hand . . . " Phrases like "a controversial issue" are so commonly used and recycled that they are generic—community property that can be freely used without fear of committing plagiarism. It *is* plagiarism, however, if the words used to fill in the blanks of such formulas are borrowed from others without proper acknowledgment. In sum, then, while it is not plagiarism to recycle conventionally used formulas, it is a serious academic offense to take the substantive content from others' texts without citing the author and giving him or her proper credit.

PUTTING IN YOUR OAR

Though the immediate goal of this book is to help you become a better writer, at a deeper level it invites you to become a certain type of person: a critical, intellectual thinker who, instead of sitting passively on the sidelines, can participate in the debates and conversations of your world in an active and empowered way. Ultimately, this book invites you to become a critical thinker who can enter the types of conversations described eloquently by the philosopher Kenneth Burke in the following widely cited passage. Likening the world of intellectual exchange to a never-ending conversation at a party, Burke writes:

> You come late. When you arrive, others have long preceded you, and they are engaged in a heated discussion, a discussion too heated for them to pause and tell you exactly what it is about. . . . You listen for a while, until you decide that you have caught the tenor of the argument; then you put in your oar. Someone answers; you answer him; another comes to your defense; another aligns himself against you. . . . The hour grows late, you must depart. And you do depart, with the discussion still vigorously in progress.
>
> KENNETH BURKE, *The Philosophy of Literary Form*

What we like about this passage is its suggestion that stating an argument and "putting in your oar" can only be done in conversation with others; that we all enter the dynamic world of ideas not as isolated individuals but as social beings deeply connected to others who have a stake in what we say.

This ability to enter complex, many-sided conversations has taken on a special urgency in today's diverse, post-9/11 world, where the future for all of us may depend on our ability to put ourselves in the shoes of those who think very differently from us. The central piece of advice in this book—that we listen carefully to others, including those who disagree with us, and then engage with them thoughtfully and respectfully—can help us see beyond our own pet beliefs, which may not be shared by everyone. The mere act of crafting a sentence that begins "Of course, someone might object that _____" may not seem like a way to change the world; but it does have the potential to jog us out of our comfort zones, to get us thinking critically about our own beliefs, and perhaps even to change our minds.

Exercises

1. Read the following paragraph from an essay by Emily Poe, a student at Furman University. Disregarding for the moment what Poe says, focus your attention on the phrases Poe uses to structure what she says (italicized here). Then write a new paragraph using Poe's as a model but replacing her topic, vegetarianism, with one of your own.

   The term "vegetarian" tends to be synonymous with "tree-hugger" in many people's minds. *They see* vegetarianism as a cult that brainwashes its followers into eliminating an essential part of their daily diets for an abstract goal of "animal welfare." *However*, few vege-tarians choose their lifestyle just to follow the crowd. *On the con-trary*, many of these supposedly brainwashed people are actually independent thinkers, concerned citizens, and compassionate human beings. *For the truth is* that there are many very good rea-sons for giving up meat. Perhaps the best reasons are to improve the environment, to encourage humane treatment of livestock, or to enhance one's own health. *In this essay, then*, closely examining a vegetarian diet as compared to a meat-eater's diet will show that vegetarianism is clearly the better option for sustaining the Earth and all its inhabitants.

2. Write a short essay in which you first summarize our ration-ale for the templates in this book and then articulate your own position in response. If you want, you can use the tem-plate below to organize your paragraphs, expanding and modifying it as necessary to fit what you want to say.

> ▸ In the Introduction to *"They Say / I Say": The Moves That Mat-ter in Academic Writing*, Gerald Graff and Cathy Birkenstein pro-vide templates designed to _____. Specifically, Graff and Birkenstein argue that the types of writing templates they offer _____. As the authors themselves put it, "_____." Although some people believe _____, Graff and Birkenstein insist that _____. In sum, then, their view is that _____.
>
> I [agree/disagree/have mixed feelings]. In my view, the types of templates that the authors recommend _____. For instance, _____. In addition, _____. Some might object, of course, on the grounds that _____. Yet I would argue that _____. Overall, then, I believe _____ —an important point to make given _____.

1

"THEY SAY"

ONE

"THEY SAY"

Starting with What Others Are Saying

—⌐⌐—

NOT LONG AGO we attended a talk at an academic confer-ence where the speaker's central claim seemed to be that a certain sociologist—call him Dr. X—had done very good work in a number of areas of the discipline. The speaker proceeded to illustrate his thesis by referring extensively and in great detail to various books and articles by Dr. X and by quoting long passages from them. The speaker was obviously both learned and impassioned, but as we listened to his talk we found ourselves somewhat puzzled: the argument—that Dr. X's work was very important—was clear enough, but why did the speaker need to make it in the first place? Did anyone dispute it? Were there commentators in the field who had argued against X's work or challenged its value? Was the speaker's interpretation of what X had done somehow novel or revolu-tionary? Since the speaker gave no hint of an answer to any of these questions, we could only wonder why he was going on and on about X. It was only after the speaker finished and took questions from the audience that we got a clue: in response to one ques-tioner, he referred to several critics who had vigorously

The hypo-thetical audience in Figure 1 on p. 4 reacts similarly.

questioned Dr. X's ideas and convinced many sociologists that Dr. X's work was unsound.

This story illustrates an important lesson: that to give writing the most important thing of all—namely, a point—a writer needs to indicate clearly not only what his or her thesis is, but also what larger conversation that thesis is responding to. Because our speaker failed to mention what others had said about Dr. X's work, he left his audience unsure about why he felt the need to say what he was saying. Perhaps the point was clear to other sociologists in the audience who were more familiar with the debates over Dr. X's work than we were. But even they, we bet, would have understood the speaker's point better if he'd sketched in some of the larger conversation his own claims were a part of and reminded the audience about what "they say."

This story also illustrates an important lesson about the *order* in which things are said: to keep an audience engaged, a writer needs to explain what he or she is responding to—either before offering that response or, at least, very early in the discussion. Delaying this explanation for more than one or two paragraphs in a very short essay, three or four pages in a longer one, or more than ten or so pages in a book-length text reverses the natural order in which readers process material—and in which writers think and develop ideas. After all, it seems very unlikely that our conference speaker first developed his defense of Dr. X and only later came across Dr. X's critics. As someone knowledgeable in his field, the speaker surely encountered the criticisms first and only then was compelled to respond and, as he saw it, set the record straight.

Therefore, when it comes to constructing an argument (whether orally or in writing), we offer you the following advice: remember that you are entering a conversation and therefore need to start with "what others are saying," as the title of this chapter recommends, and then introduce your own ideas as a response. Specifically, we suggest that you summarize what "they say" as soon as you can in your text, and remind readers of it at strategic points as your text unfolds. Though it's true that not all texts follow this practice, we think it's important for all writers to master it before they depart from it.

This is not to say that you must start with a detailed list of everyone who has written on your subject before you offer your own ideas. Had our conference speaker gone to the opposite extreme and spent most of his talk summarizing Dr. X's critics with no hint of what he himself had to say, the audience probably would have had the same frustrated "why-is-he-going-on-like-this?" reaction. What we suggest, then, is that as soon as possible you state your own position and the one it's responding to *together*, and that you think of the two as a unit. It is generally best to summarize the ideas you're responding to briefly, at the start of your text, and to delay detailed elaboration until later. The point is to give your readers a quick preview of what is motivating your argument, not to drown them in details right away.

Starting with a summary of others' views may seem to contradict the common advice that writers should lead with their own thesis or claim. Although we agree that you shouldn't keep readers in suspense too long about your central argument, we also believe that you need to present that argument as part of some larger conversation, indicating something about the arguments of others that you are supporting, opposing, amending, complicating, or qualifying. One added benefit of summarizing others' views as soon as you can: you let those others do some of the work of framing and clarifying the issue you're writing about.

Consider, for example, how George Orwell starts his famous essay "Politics and the English Language" with what others are saying.

Most people who bother with the matter at all would admit that the English language is in a bad way, but it is generally assumed that we cannot by conscious action do anything about it. Our civilization is decadent and our language—so the argument runs—must inevitably share in the general collapse. . . .

[But] the process is reversible. Modern English . . . is full of bad habits . . . which can be avoided if one is willing to take the necessary trouble.

GEORGE ORWELL, "Politics and the English Language"

Orwell is basically saying, "Most people assume that we cannot do anything about the bad state of the English language. But I say we can."

Of course, there are many other powerful ways to begin. Instead of opening with someone else's views, you could start with an illustrative quotation, a revealing fact or statistic, or—as we do in this chapter—a relevant anecdote. If you choose one of these formats, however, be sure that it in some way illustrates the view you're addressing or leads you to that view directly, with a minimum of steps.

In opening this chapter, for example, we devote the first paragraph to an anecdote about the conference speaker and then move quickly at the start of the second paragraph to the misconception about writing exemplified by the speaker. In the following opening, from a 2004 opinion piece in the *New York Times Book Review*, Christina Nehring also moves quickly from an anecdote illustrating something she dislikes to her own claim—that book lovers think too highly of themselves.

"I'm a reader!" announced the yellow button. "How about you?" I looked at its bearer, a strapping young guy stalking my town's Festival of Books. "I'll bet you're a reader," he volunteered, as though we were two geniuses well met. "No," I replied. "Absolutely not," I wanted to yell, and fling my Barnes & Noble bag at his feet. Instead, I mumbled something apologetic and melted into the crowd.

There's a new piety in the air: the self congratulation of book lovers.

CHRISTINA NEHRING, "Books Make You a Boring Person"

Nehring's anecdote is really a kind of "they say": book lovers keep telling themselves how great they are.

TEMPLATES FOR INTRODUCING WHAT "THEY SAY"

There are lots of conventional ways to introduce what others are saying. Here are some standard templates that we would have recommended to our conference speaker.

▸ A number of sociologists have recently suggested <u>that X's work has several fundamental problems</u>.

▸ It has become common today to dismiss ＿＿＿＿＿.

▸ In their recent work, Y and Z have offered harsh critiques of ＿＿＿＿ for ＿＿＿＿.

TEMPLATES FOR INTRODUCING "STANDARD VIEWS"

The following templates can help you make what we call the "standard view" move, in which you introduce a view that has become so widely accepted that by now it is essentially the conventional way of thinking about a topic.

- Americans have always believed that <u>individual effort can triumph over circumstances</u>.

- Conventional wisdom has it that _____.

- Common sense seems to dictate that _____.

- The standard way of thinking about topic X has it that _____.

- It is often said that _____.

- My whole life I have heard it said that _____.

- You would think that _____.

- Many people assume that _____.

These templates are popular because they provide a quick and efficient way to perform one of the most common moves that writers make: challenging widely accepted beliefs, placing them on the examining table and analyzing their strengths and weaknesses.

TEMPLATES FOR MAKING WHAT "THEY SAY" SOMETHING *YOU* SAY

Another way to introduce the views you're responding to is to present them as your own. That is, the "they say" that you respond to need not be a view held by others; it can be one that you yourself once held or one that you are ambivalent about.

- I've always believed that <u>museums are boring</u>.

- When I was a child, I used to think that _____.

▸ Although I should know better by now, I cannot help thinking that ＿＿＿＿＿ .

▸ At the same time that I believe ＿＿＿＿＿ , I also believe ＿＿＿＿＿ .

TEMPLATES FOR INTRODUCING SOMETHING IMPLIED OR ASSUMED

Another sophisticated move a writer can make is to summarize a point that is not directly stated in what "they say" but is implied or assumed.

▸ Although none of them have ever said so directly, my teachers have often given me the impression that <u>education will open doors</u>.

▸ One implication of X's treatment of ＿＿＿＿＿ is that ＿＿＿＿＿ .

▸ X apparently assumes that ＿＿＿＿＿ .

▸ While they rarely admit as much, ＿＿＿＿＿ often take for granted that ＿＿＿＿＿ .

These are templates that can help you think analytically— to look beyond what others say explicitly and to consider their unstated assumptions, as well as the implications of their views.

TEMPLATES FOR INTRODUCING AN ONGOING DEBATE

Sometimes you'll want to open by summarizing a debate that presents two or more views. This kind of opening demonstrates your awareness that there are conflicting ways to look at your subject, the clear mark of someone who knows the subject and therefore is likely to be a reliable, trustworthy guide. Furthermore, opening with a summary of a debate can help you explore the issue you are writing about before declaring your own view. In this way, you can use the writing process itself to help you discover where you stand instead of having to commit to a position before you are ready to do so.

Here is a basic template for opening with a debate.

> ▸ In discussions of X, one controversial issue has been _____.
> On the one hand, _____ argues _____.
> On the other hand, _____ contends _____. Others
> even maintain _____. My own view is _____.

The cognitive scientist Mark Aronoff uses this kind of template in an essay on the workings of the human brain.

> Theories of how the mind/brain works have been dominated for centuries by two opposing views. One, rationalism, sees the human mind as coming into this world more or less fully formed—preprogrammed, in modern terms. The other, empiricism, sees the mind of the newborn as largely unstructured, a blank slate.
>
> MARK ARONOFF, "Washington Sleeped Here"

Another way to open with a debate involves starting with a proposition many people agree with in order to highlight the point(s) on which they ultimately disagree.

> ▸ When it comes to the topic of _____, most of us will readily
> agree that _____. Where this agreement usually

ends, however, is on the question of _____ . Whereas
some are convinced that _____ , others maintain that
_____ .

The political writer Thomas Frank uses a variation on this
move.

> That we are a nation divided is an almost universal lament of this
> bitter election year. However, the exact property that divides us—
> elemental though it is said to be—remains a matter of some
> controversy.
>
> THOMAS FRANK, "American Psyche"

KEEP WHAT "THEY SAY" IN VIEW

We can't urge you too strongly to keep in mind what "they say"
as you move through the rest of your text. After summarizing
the ideas you are responding to at the outset, it's very important to continue to keep those ideas in view. Readers won't be
able to follow your unfolding response, much less any complications you may offer, unless you keep reminding them what
claims you are responding to.

In other words, even when presenting your own claims,
you should keep returning to the motivating "they say." The
longer and more complicated your text, the greater the
chance that readers will forget what ideas originally motivated it—no matter how clearly you lay them out at the
beginning. At strategic moments throughout your text, we
recommend that you include what we call "return sentences."
Here is an example.

▸ In conclusion, then, as I suggested earlier, defenders of
_____ can't have it both ways. Their assertion that _____
is contradicted by their claim that _____.

We ourselves use such return sentences at every opportunity in
this book to remind you of the view of writing that our book
questions—that good writing means making true or smart or
logical statements about a given subject with little or no reference to what others say about it.

By reminding readers of the ideas you're responding to,
return sentences ensure that your text maintains a sense of mission and urgency from start to finish. In short, they help ensure
that your argument is a genuine response to others' views rather
than just a set of observations about a given subject. The difference is huge. To be responsive to others and the conversation you're entering, you need to start with what others are
saying and continue keeping it in the reader's view.

Exercises

1. The following is a list of arguments that lack a "they say"—
   any sense of who needs to hear these claims, who might
   think otherwise. Like the speaker in the cartoon on page 4
   who declares that *The Sopranos* presents complex characters,
   these one-sided arguments fail to explain what view they are
   responding to—what view, in effect, they are trying to correct, add to, qualify, complicate, and so forth. Your job in
   this exercise is to provide each argument with such a counterview. Feel free to use any of the templates in this chapter that you find helpful.

a. Our experiments suggest that there are dangerous levels of chemical X in the Ohio groundwater.

b. Material forces drive history.

c. Proponents of Freudian psychology question standard notions of "rationality."

d. Male students often dominate class discussions.

e. The film is about the problems of romantic relationships.

f. I'm afraid that templates like the ones in this book will stifle my creativity.

2. Below is a template that we derived from the opening of David Zinczenko's "Don't Blame the Eater" (p. 195). Use the template to structure a passage on a topic of your own choosing. Your first step here should be to find an idea that you support that others not only disagree with but actually find laughable (or, as Zinczenko puts it, worthy of a Jay Leno monologue). You might write about one of the topics listed in the previous exercise (the environment, sports, gender relations, the meaning of a book or movie) or any other topic that interests you.

▸ If ever there was an idea custom-made for a Jay Leno monologue, this was it: _____, Isn't that like _____?
Whatever happened to _____?

   I happen to sympathize with _____, though,
perhaps because

TWO

"HER POINT IS"

The Art of Summarizing

———⊡———

IF IT IS TRUE, as we claim in this book, that to argue persuasively you need to be in dialogue with others, then summarizing others' arguments is central to your arsenal of basic moves. Because writers who make strong claims need to map their claims relative to those of other people, it is important to know how to summarize effectively what those other people say. (We're using the word "summarizing" here to refer to any information from others that you present in your own words, including that which you paraphrase.)

Many writers shy away from summarizing—perhaps because they don't want to take the trouble to go back to the text in question and wrestle with what it says, or because they fear that devoting too much time to other people's ideas will take away from their own. When assigned to write a response to an article, such writers might offer their own views on the article's *topic* while hardly mentioning what the article itself argues or says. At the opposite extreme are those who do nothing *but* summarize. Lacking confidence, perhaps, in their own ideas, these writers so overload their texts with summaries of others' ideas that their own voice gets lost. And since these summaries are not animated by the writers' own interests, they often read like mere lists of things that X thinks or Y says—with no clear focus.

As a general rule, a good summary requires balancing what the original author is saying with the writer's own focus. Generally speaking, a summary must at once be true to what the original author says while also emphasizing those aspects of what the author says that interest you, the writer. Striking this delicate balance can be tricky, since it means facing two ways at once: both outward (toward the author being summarized) and inward (toward yourself). Ultimately, it means being respectful of others but simultaneously structuring how you summarize them in light of your own text's central claim.

On the One Hand, Put Yourself in *Their* Shoes

To write a really good summary, you must be able to suspend your own beliefs for a time and put yourself in the shoes of someone else. This means playing what the writing theorist Peter Elbow calls the "believing game," in which you try to inhabit the world-view of those whose conversation you are joining—and whom you are perhaps even disagreeing with—and try to see their argument from their perspective. This ability to temporarily suspend one's own convictions is a hallmark of good actors, who must convincingly "become" characters whom in real life they may detest. As a writer, when you play the believing game well, readers should not be able to tell whether you agree or disagree with the ideas you are summarizing.

If, as a writer, you cannot or will not suspend your own beliefs in this way, you are likely to produce summaries that are so obviously biased that they undermine your credibility with readers. Consider the following summary.

> David Zinczenko's article, "Don't Blame the Eater," is nothing more than an angry rant in which he accuses the fast-food companies of an evil conspiracy to make people fat. I disagree because these companies have to make money. . . .

If you review what Zinczenko actually says (pp. 139–41), you should immediately see that this summary amounts to an unfair distortion. While Zinczenko does argue that the practices of the fast-food industry have the *effect* of making people fat, his tone is never "angry," and he never goes so far as to suggest that the fast-food industry conspires to make people fat with deliberately evil intent.

Another tell-tale sign of this writer's failure to give Zinczenko a fair hearing is the hasty way he abandons the summary after only one sentence and rushes on to his own response. So eager is this writer to disagree that he not only caricatures what Zinczenko says but also gives the article a hasty, superficial reading. Granted, there are many writing situations in which, because of matters of proportion, a one- or two-sentence summary is precisely what you want. Indeed, as writing professor Karen Lunsford (whose own research focuses on argument theory) points out, it is standard in the natural and social sciences to summarize the work of others quickly, in one pithy sentence or phrase, as in the following example.

> Several studies (Crackle, 1992; Pop, 2001; Snap, 1987) suggest that these policies are harmless; moreover, other studies (Dick, 2002; Harry, 2003; Tom, 1987) argue that they even have benefits.

But if your assignment is to respond in writing to a single author like Zinczenko, you will need to tell your readers enough about his or her argument so they can assess its merits on their own, independent of you.

When a writer fails to provide enough summary or to engage in a rigorous or serious enough summary, he or she often falls prey to what we call "the closest cliché syndrome," in which what gets summarized is not the view the author in question has actually expressed but a familiar cliché that the writer *mistakes* for the author's view (sometimes because the writer believes it and mistakenly assumes the author must too). So, for example, Martin Luther King Jr.'s passionate defense of civil disobedience in "Letter from Birmingham Jail" might be summarized not as the defense of political protest that it actually is but as a plea for everyone to "just get along." Similarly, Zinczenko's critique of the fast-food industry might be summarized as a call for overweight people to take responsibility for their weight.

Whenever you enter into a conversation with others in your writing, then, it is extremely important that you go back to what those others have said, that you study it very closely, and that you not confuse it with something you already believe. A writer who fails to do this ends up essentially conversing with imaginary others who are really only the products of his or her own biases and preconceptions.

ON THE OTHER HAND, KNOW WHERE *YOU* ARE GOING

Even as writing an effective summary requires you to temporarily adopt the worldview of another, it does not mean ignoring your own view altogether. Paradoxically, at the same time that summarizing another text requires you to represent fairly what it says, it also requires that your own response exert a quiet influence. A good summary, in other words, has a focus or spin that allows the summary to fit with your own agenda while still being true to the text you are summarizing.

Thus if you are writing in response to the essay by Zinczenko, you should be able to see that an essay on the fast-food industry in general will call for a very different summary than will an essay on parenting, corporate regulation, or warning labels. If you want your essay to encompass all three topics, you'll need to subordinate these three issues to one of Zinczenko's general claims and then make sure this general claim directly sets up your own argument.

For example, suppose you want to argue that it is parents, not fast-food companies, who are to blame for children's obesity. To set up this argument, you will probably want to compose a summary that highlights what Zinczenko says about the fast-food industry *and parents*. Consider this sample.

In his article "Don't Blame the Eater," David Zinczenko blames the fast-food industry for fueling today's so-called obesity epidemic, not only by failing to provide adequate warning labels on its high-calorie foods but also by filling the nutritional void in children's lives left by their overtaxed working parents. With many parents working long hours and unable to supervise what their children eat, Zinczenko claims, children today are easily victimized by the low-cost, calorie-laden foods that the fast-food chains are all too eager to supply. When he was a young boy, for instance, and his single mother was away at work, he ate at Taco Bell, McDonald's, and other chains on a regular basis, and ended up overweight. Zinczenko's hope is that with the new spate of lawsuits against the food industry, other children with working parents will have healthier choices available to them, and that they will not, like him, become obese.

In my view, however, it is the parents, and not the food chains, who are responsible for their children's obesity. While it is true that many of today's parents work long hours, there are still several things that parents can do to guarantee that their children eat healthy foods. . . .

The summary in the first paragraph succeeds because it points in two directions at once—both toward Zinczenko's own text *and* toward the second paragraph, where the writer begins to establish her own argument. The opening sentence gives a sense of Zinczenko's general argument (that the fast-food chains are to blame for obesity), including his two main supporting claims (about warning labels and parents), but it ends with an emphasis on the writer's main concern: parental responsibility. In this way, the summary does justice to Zinczenko's arguments while also setting up the ensuing critique.

This advice—to summarize authors in light of your own arguments—may seem painfully obvious. But writers often summarize a given author on one issue even though their text actually focuses on another. To avoid this problem, you need to make sure that your "they say" and "I say" are well matched. In fact, aligning what they say with what you say is a good thing to work on when revising what you've written.

Often writers who summarize without regard to their own interests fall prey to what might be called "list summaries," summaries that simply inventory the original author's various points but fail to focus those points around any larger overall claim. If you've ever heard a talk in which the points were connected only by words like "and then," "also," and "in addition," you

THE EFFECT OF A TYPICAL LIST SUMMARY

FIGURE 3

know how such lists can put listeners to sleep—as shown in Figure 3. A typical list summary sounds like this.

> The author says many different things about his subject. *First* he says. . . . *Then* he makes the point that. . . . *In addition* he says. . . . *And then* he writes. . . . *Also* he shows that. . . . *And then* he says. . . .

It may be boring list summaries like this that give summaries in general a bad name and even prompt some instructors to discourage their students from summarizing at all.

In conclusion, writing a good summary means not just representing an author's view accurately, but doing so in a way that fits your own composition's larger agenda. On the one hand, it means playing Peter Elbow's believing game and doing justice to the source; if the summary ignores or misrepresents the source, its bias and unfairness will show. On the other hand, even as it does justice to the source, a summary has to have a slant or spin that prepares the way for your own claims. Once a summary enters your text, you should think of it as joint property—reflecting both the source you are summarizing and your own views.

SUMMARIZING SATIRICALLY

Thus far in this chapter we have argued that, as a general rule, good summaries require a balance between what someone else has said and your own interests as a writer. Now, however, we want to address one exception to this rule: the satiric summary, in which a writer deliberately gives his or her own spin to someone else's argument in order to reveal a glaring shortcoming in it. Despite our previous comments that well-crafted summaries generally strike a balance between heeding what someone else has said and your own independent interests, the satiric mode can at times be a very effective form of critique because it lets the summarized argument condemn itself without overt editorializing by you, the writer. If you've ever watched *The Daily Show*, you'll recall that it often merely summarizes silly things political leaders have said or done, letting their words or actions undermine themselves.

Consider another example. In late September 2001, former President George W. Bush in a speech to Congress urged the nation's "continued participation and confidence in the American economy" as a means of recovering from the terrorist attacks of 9/11. The journalist Allan Sloan criticized this proposal simply by summarizing it, observing that the president had equated "patriotism with shopping. Maxing out your credit cards at the mall wasn't self indulgence, it was a way to get back at Osama bin Laden." Sloan's summary leaves no doubt where he stands—he considers Bush's proposal ridiculous, or at least too simple.

USE SIGNAL VERBS THAT FIT THE ACTION

In introducing summaries, try to avoid bland formulas like "she says," or "they believe." Though language like this is sometimes serviceable enough, it often fails to reflect accurately what's been said. In some cases, "he says" may even drain the passion out of the ideas you're summarizing.

We suspect that the habit of ignoring the action in what we summarize stems from the mistaken belief we mentioned earlier that writing is about playing it safe and not making waves, a matter of piling up truths and bits of knowledge rather than a dynamic process of doing things to and with other people. People who wouldn't hesitate to *say* "X totally misrepresented," "attacked," or "loved" something when chatting with friends will in their writing often opt for far tamer and even less accurate phrases like "X said."

But the authors you summarize at the college level seldom simply "say" or "discuss" things; they "urge," "emphasize," and "complain about" them. David Zinczenko, for example, doesn't just *say* that fast-food companies contribute to obesity; he *complains* or *protests* that they do; he *challenges*, *chastises*, and *indicts* those companies. The Declaration of Independence doesn't just *talk about* the treatment of the colonies by the British; it *protests against* it. To do justice to the authors you cite, we recommend that when summarizing—or when introducing a quotation—you use vivid and precise signal verbs as often as possible. Though "he says" or "she believes" will sometimes be the most appropriate language for the occasion, your text will often be more accurate and lively if you tailor your verbs to suit the precise actions you're describing.

TEMPLATES FOR INTRODUCING SUMMARIES AND QUOTATIONS

▸ She advocates a radical revision of the juvenile justice system.

▸ They celebrate the fact that   .

▸   , he admits.

VERBS FOR INTRODUCING SUMMARIES AND QUOTATIONS

VERBS FOR MAKING A CLAIM

argue	insist
assert	observe
believe	remind us
claim	report
emphasize	suggest

VERBS FOR EXPRESSING AGREEMENT

acknowledge	endorse
admire	extol
agree	praise

VERBS FOR EXPRESSING AGREEMENT

celebrate the fact that	reaffirm
corroborate	support
do not deny	verify

VERBS FOR QUESTIONING OR DISAGREEING

complain	qualify
complicate	question
contend	refute
contradict	reject
deny	renounce
deplore the tendency to	repudiate

VERBS FOR MAKING RECOMMENDATIONS

advocate	implore
call for	plead
demand	recommend
encourage	urge
exhort	warn

Exercises

1. To get a feel for Peter Elbow's "believing game," write a summary of some belief that you strongly disagree with. Then write a summary of the position that you actually hold on this topic. Give both summaries to a classmate or two, and see if they can tell which position you endorse. If you've succeeded, they won't be able to tell.

2. Write two different summaries of David Zinczenko's "Don't Blame the Eater" (pp. 195–97). Write the first one for an essay arguing that, contrary to what Zinczenko claims, there *are* inexpensive and convenient alternatives to fast-food restaurants. Write the second for an essay that questions whether being overweight is a genuine medical problem rather than a problem of cultural stereotypes. Compare your two summaries: though they are about the same article, they should look very different.

THREE

"As He Himself Puts It"

The Art of Quoting

—◻—

A KEY PREMISE of this book is that to launch an effective argument you need to write the arguments of others into your text. One of the best ways to do so is by not only summarizing what "they say," as suggested in Chapter 2, but by quoting their exact words. Quoting someone else's words gives a tremendous amount of credibility to your summary and helps ensure that it is fair and accurate. In a sense, then, quotations function as a kind of proof of evidence, saying to readers: "Look, I'm not just making this up. She makes this claim and here it is in her exact words."

Yet many writers make a host of mistakes when it comes to quoting, not the least of which is the failure to quote enough in the first place, if at all. Some writers quote too little— perhaps because they don't want to bother going back to the original text and looking up the author's exact words, or because they think they can reconstruct the author's ideas from memory. At the opposite extreme are writers who so overquote that they end up with texts that are short on commentary of their own—maybe because they lack confidence in their ability to comment on the quotations, or because they don't fully understand what they've quoted and therefore have trouble explaining what the quotations mean.

But the main problem with quoting arises when writers assume that quotations speak for themselves. Because the meaning of a quotation is obvious to *them*, many writers assume that this meaning will also be obvious to their readers, when often it is not. Writers who make this mistake think that their job is done when they've chosen a quotation and inserted it into their text. They draft an essay, slap in a few quotations, and whammo, they're done.

Such writers fail to see that quoting means more than simply enclosing what "they say" in quotation marks. In a way, quotations are orphans: words that have been taken from their original contexts and that need to be integrated into their new textual surroundings. This chapter offers two key ways to produce this sort of integration: (1) by choosing quotations wisely, with an eye to how well they support a particular part of your text, and (2) by surrounding every major quotation with a frame explaining whose words they are, what the quotation means, and how the quotation relates to your own text. The point we want to emphasize is that quoting what "they say" must always be connected with what *you* say.

QUOTE RELEVANT PASSAGES

Before you can select appropriate quotations, you need to have a sense of what you want to do with them—that is, how they will support your text at the particular point where you insert them. Be careful not to select quotations just for the sake of demonstrating that you've read the author's work; you need to make sure they support your own argument.

However, finding relevant quotations is not always easy. In fact, sometimes quotations that were initially relevant to your argument, or to a key point in it, become less so as your text changes during the process of writing and revising. Given the evolving and messy nature of writing, you may sometimes think that you've found the perfect quotation to support your argument, only to discover later on, as your text develops, that your focus has changed and the quotation no longer works. It can be somewhat misleading, then, to speak of finding your thesis and finding relevant quotations as two separate steps, one coming after the other. When you're deeply engaged in the writing and revising process, there is usually a great deal of back-and-forth between your argument and any quotations you select.

FRAME EVERY QUOTATION

Finding relevant quotations is only part of your job; you also need to present them in a way that makes their relevance and meaning clear to your readers. Since quotations do not speak for themselves, you need to build a frame around them in which you do that speaking for them.

Quotations that are inserted into a text without such a frame are sometimes called "dangling" quotations for the way they're left dangling without any explanation. One former graduate teaching assistant we worked with, Steve Benton, calls these "hit-and-run" quotations, likening them to car accidents in which the driver speeds away and avoids taking responsibility for the dent in your fender or the smashed taillights, as in Figure 4.

On the following page is a typical hit-and-run quotation by a writer responding to an essay by the feminist philoso-

DON'T BE A HIT-AND-RUN QUOTER.

FIGURE 4

pher Susan Bordo, who laments that media pressures on young women to diet are spreading to previously isolated regions of the world like the Fiji islands.

> Susan Bordo writes about women and dieting. "Fiji is just one example. Until television was introduced in 1995, the islands had no reported cases of eating disorders. In 1998, three years after programs from the United States and Britain began broadcasting there, 62 percent of the girls surveyed reported dieting."
>
> I think Bordo is right. Another point Bordo makes is that. . . .

Since this writer fails to introduce the quotation adequately or explain why he finds it worth quoting, readers will have a hard time reconstructing what Bordo argued. Besides neglecting to say who Bordo is or even that the quoted words are hers, the writer does not explain how her words connect with anything he is saying or even what she says that he thinks is so "right." He simply abandons the quotation in his haste to zoom on to another point.

To adequately frame a quotation, you need to insert it into what we like to call a "quotation sandwich," with the statement introducing it serving as the top slice of bread and the explanation following it serving as the bottom slice. The introductory or lead-in claims should explain who is speaking and set up what the quotation says; the follow-up statements should explain why you consider the quotation to be important and what you take it to say.

TEMPLATES FOR INTRODUCING QUOTATIONS

▸ X states, "not all steroids should be banned from sports."

▸ As the prominent philosopher X puts it, "_____."

▸ According to X, "_____."

▸ X himself writes, "_____."

▸ In her book, _____, X maintains that "_____."

▸ Writing in the journal *Commentary*, X complains that "_____."

▸ In X's view, "_____."

▸ X agrees when she writes, "_____."

▸ X disagrees when he writes, "_____."

▸ X complicates matters further when she writes, "_____."

TEMPLATES FOR EXPLAINING QUOTATIONS

The one piece of advice about quoting that our students say they find most helpful is to get in the habit of following every major quotation by explaining what it means, using a template like one of the ones below.

▸ Basically, X is warning that the proposed solution will only make the problem worse.

▸ In other words, X believes _____.

▸ In making this comment, X urges us to _____.

▸ X is corroborating the age-old adage that _____.

▸ X's point is that _____.

▸ The essence of X's argument is that _____.

When offering such explanations, it is important to use language that accurately reflects the spirit of the quoted passage. It is quite serviceable to write "Bordo states" or "asserts" in introducing the quotation about Fiji. But given the fact that Bordo is clearly alarmed by the extension of the media's reach to Fiji, it is far more accurate to use language that reflects her alarm: "Bordo is alarmed that" or "is disturbed by" or "complains."

See pp. 39–40 for a list of action verbs for summarizing what others say.

Consider, for example, how the earlier passage on Bordo might be revised using some of these moves.

The feminist philosopher Susan Bordo deplores Western media's obsession with female thinness and dieting. Her basic complaint is that increasing numbers of women across the globe are being led to see themselves as fat and in need of a diet. Citing the islands of Fiji as a case in point, Bordo notes that "until television was introduced in 1995, the islands had no reported cases of eating disorders. In 1998, three years after programs from the United States

and Britain began broadcasting there, 62 percent of the girls sur-
veyed reported dieting" (149–50). Bordo's point is that the Western cult of dieting is spreading even to remote places across the
globe. Ultimately, Bordo complains, the culture of dieting will find
you, regardless of where you live.

Bordo's observations ring true to me because, now that I think
about it, most women I know, regardless of where they are from,
are seriously unhappy with their weight. . . .

This framing of the quotation not only better integrates Bordo's
words into the writer's text, but also serves to demonstrate the
writer's interpretation of what Bordo is saying. While "the feminist philosopher" and "Bordo notes" provide information that
readers need to know, the sentences that follow the quotation
build a bridge between Bordo's words and those of the writer.
The reference to 62 percent of Fijian girls dieting is no longer
an inert statistic (as it was in the flawed passage presented
earlier) but a quantitative example of how "the Western cult
of dieting is spreading . . . across the globe." Just as important, these sentences explain what Bordo is saying in the
writer's own words—and thereby make clear that the quotation is being used purposefully to set up the writer's own argument and has not been stuck in just for padding the essay or
the works-cited list.

BLEND THE AUTHOR'S WORDS
WITH YOUR OWN

The above framing material also works well because it accurately represents Bordo's words while giving those words the
writer's own spin. Notice how the passage refers several times

to the key concept of dieting, and how it echoes Bordo's references to "television" and to U.S. and British "broadcasting" by referring to "culture," which is further specified as "Western." Instead of simply repeating Bordo word for word, the follow-up sentences echo just enough of her language while still moving the discussion in the writer's own direction. In effect, the framing creates a kind of hybrid mix of Bordo's words and those of the writer.

CAN YOU OVERANALYZE A QUOTATION?

But is it possible to overexplain a quotation? And how do you know when you've explained a quotation thoroughly enough? After all, not all quotations require the same amount of explanatory framing, and there are no hard-and-fast rules for knowing how much explanation any quotation needs. As a general rule, the most explanatory framing is needed for quotations that may be hard for readers to process: quotations that are long and complex, that are filled with details or jargon, or that contain hidden complexities.

And yet, though the particular situation usually dictates when and how much to explain a quotation, we will still offer one piece of advice: when in doubt, go for it. It is better to risk being overly explicit about what you take a quotation to mean than to leave the quotation dangling and your readers in doubt. Indeed, we encourage you to provide such explanatory framing even when writing to an audience that you know to be familiar with the author being quoted and able to interpret your quotations on their own. Even in such cases, readers need to see how *you* interpret the quotation, since words—especially those of controversial figures—can be interpreted in various ways and used to support different, sometimes opposing, agendas. Your readers need to see what you make of the material you've quoted, if only to be sure that your reading of the material and theirs is on the same page.

How *Not* to Introduce Quotations

We want to conclude this chapter by surveying some ways *not* to introduce quotations. Although some writers do so, you should not introduce quotations by saying something like "Orwell asserts an idea that" or "A quote by Shakespeare says." Introductory phrases like these are both redundant and misleading. In the first example, you could write either "Orwell asserts that" or "Orwell's assertion is that," rather than redundantly combining the two. The second example misleads readers, since it is the writer who is doing the quoting, not Shakespeare (as "a quote by Shakespeare" implies).

The templates in this book will help you avoid such mistakes. Once you have mastered templates like "as X puts it," or "in X's own words," you probably won't even have to think about them—and will be free to focus on the challenging ideas that templates help you frame.

Exercises

1. Find a published piece of writing that quotes something that "they say." How has the writer integrated the quotation into his or her own text? How has he or she introduced the quotation, and what, if anything, has the writer said to explain it and tie it to his or her own text? Based on what you've read in this chapter, are there any changes you would suggest?

2. Look at something you have written for one of your classes. Have you quoted any sources? If so, how have you integrated the quotation into your own text? How have you introduced it? Explained what it means? Indicated how it relates to *your* text? If you haven't done all these things, revise your text to do so, perhaps using the Templates for Introducing Quotations (p. 46) and Explaining Quotations (pp. 46–47). If you've not written anything with quotations, try revising some academic text you've written to do so.

2

"I Say"

FOUR

"YES / NO / OKAY, BUT"

Three Ways to Respond

—◻—

THE FIRST THREE chapters of this book discuss the "they say" stage of writing, in which you devote your attention to the views of some other person or group. In this chapter we move to the "I say" stage, in which you offer your own argument as a response to what "they" have said.

Moving to the "I say" stage can be daunting in academia, where it often may seem that you need to be an expert in a field to have an argument at all. Many students have told us that they have trouble entering some of the high-powered conversations that take place in college or graduate school because they do not know enough about the topic at hand, or because, they say, they simply are not "smart enough." Yet often these same students, when given a chance to study in depth the contribution that some scholar has made in a given field, will turn around and say things like "I can see where she is coming from, how she makes her case by building on what other scholars have said. Perhaps had I studied the situation longer I could have come up with a similar argument." What these students came to realize is that good arguments are based not on knowledge that only a special class of experts has access to, but on everyday habits of mind that can be isolated, identified, and used by almost anyone. Though there's certainly no substitute for expertise and for knowing as much as possible about one's topic, the arguments that finally win the day are built, as the title of this chapter suggests, on some very basic rhetorical patterns that most of us use on a daily basis.

There are a great many ways to respond to others' ideas, but this chapter concentrates on the three most common and recognizable ways: agreeing, disagreeing, or some combination of both. Although each way of responding is open to endless variation, we focus on these three because readers come to any text needing to learn fairly quickly where the writer stands, and they do this by placing the writer on a mental map consisting of a few familiar options: the writer agrees with those he or she is responding to, disagrees with them, or presents some combination of both agreeing and disagreeing.

When writers take too long to declare their position relative to views they've summarized or quoted, readers get frustrated, wondering, "Is this guy agreeing or disagreeing? Is he *for* what this other person has said, *against* it, or what?" For this reason, this chapter's advice applies to reading as well as to writing. Especially with difficult texts, you need not only to find the position the writer is responding to—the "they say"—but also to determine whether the writer is agreeing with it, challenging it, or some mixture of the two.

ONLY *THREE* WAYS TO RESPOND?

Perhaps you'll worry that fitting your own response into one of these three categories will force you to oversimplify your argument or lessen its complexity, subtlety, or originality. This is certainly a serious concern for academics who are rightly skeptical of writing that is simplistic and reductive. We would argue, however, that the more complex and subtle your argument is, and the more it departs from the conventional ways people think, the more your readers will need to be able to place it on their mental map in order to process the complex details you present. That is, the complexity, subtlety, and originality of your response are more likely to stand out and be noticed if readers have a baseline sense of where you stand relative to any ideas you've cited. As you move through this chapter, we hope you'll agree that the forms of agreeing, disagreeing, and both agreeing and disagreeing that we discuss, far from being simplistic or one-dimensional, are able to accommodate a high degree of creative, complex thought.

It is always a good tactic to begin your response not by launching directly into a mass of details but by stating clearly whether you agree, disagree, or both, using a direct, no-nonsense formula such as: "I agree," "I disagree," or "I am of two minds. I agree that _____, but I cannot agree that _____." Once you have offered one of these straightforward statements (or one of the many variations discussed below), readers will have a strong grasp of your position and then be able to appreciate the complications you go on to offer as your response unfolds.

See p. 21 for suggestions on previewing where you stand.

Still, you may object that these three basic ways of responding don't cover all the options—that they ignore interpretive or analytical responses, for example. In other words, you might think that when you interpret a literary work you don't necessarily agree or disagree with anything but simply explain the work's meaning, style, or structure. Many essays about literature and the arts, it might be said, take this form—they interpret a work's meaning, thus rendering matters of agreeing or disagreeing irrelevant.

We would argue, however, that the most interesting inter-pretations in fact tend to be those that agree, disagree, or both—that instead of being offered solo, the best interpreta-tions take strong stands relative to other interpretations. In fact, there would be no reason to offer an interpretation of a work of literature or art unless you were responding to the interpre-tations or possible interpretations of others. Even when you point out features or qualities of an artistic work that others have not noticed, you are implicitly disagreeing with what those interpreters have said by pointing out that they missed or over-looked something that, in your view, is important. In any effec-tive interpretation, then, you need not only to state what you yourself take the work of art to mean but to do so relative to the interpretations of other readers—be they professional schol-ars, teachers, classmates, or even hypothetical readers (as in, "Although some readers might think that this poem is about _____, it is in fact about _____ ").

DISAGREE—AND EXPLAIN WHY

Disagreeing may seem like one of the simpler moves a writer can make, and it is often the first thing people associate with critical thinking. Disagreeing can also be the easiest way to gen-erate an essay: find something you can disagree with in what has been said or might be said about your topic, summarize it, and argue with it. But disagreement in fact poses hidden chal-lenges. You need to do more than simply assert that you dis-agree with a particular view; you also have to offer persuasive reasons *why* you disagree. After all, disagreeing means more than adding "not" to what someone else has said, more than just saying, "Although they say women's rights are improving,

I say women's rights are *not* improving." Such a response merely contradicts the view it responds to and fails to add anything interesting or new. To turn it into an argument, you need to give reasons to support what you say: because another's argument fails to take relevant factors into account; because it is based on faulty or incomplete evidence; because it rests on questionable assumptions; or because it uses flawed logic, is contradictory, or overlooks what you take to be the real issue. To move the conversation forward (and, indeed, to justify your very act of writing), you need to demonstrate that you have something to contribute.

You can even disagree by making what we call the "duh" move, in which you disagree not with the position itself but with the assumption that it is a new or stunning revelation. Here is an example of such a move, used to open a 2003 essay on the state of American schools.

> According to a recent report by some researchers at Stanford University, high school students with college aspirations "often lack crucial information on applying to college and on succeeding academically once they get there."
>
> Well, duh. . . . It shouldn't take a Stanford research team to tell us that when it comes to "succeeding academically," many students don't have a clue.
>
> GERALD GRAFF, "Trickle-Down Obfuscation"

Like all of the other moves discussed in this book, the "duh" move can be tailored to meet the needs of almost any writing situation. If you find the expression "duh" too brash to use with your intended audience, you can always dispense with the term itself and write something like "It is true that _____; but we already knew that."

TEMPLATES FOR DISAGREEING, WITH REASONS

▸ X is mistaken because she overlooks <u>recent fossil discoveries in the South</u>.

▸ X's claim that _____ rests upon the questionable assumption that _____ .

▸ I disagree with X's view that _____ because, as recent research has shown, _____ .

▸ X contradicts herself/can't have it both ways. On the one hand, she argues _____ . On the other hand, she also says _____ .

▸ By focusing on _____ , X overlooks the deeper problem of _____ .

You can also disagree by making what we call the "twist it" move, in which you agree with the evidence that someone else has presented but show through a twist of logic that this evidence actually supports your own, contrary position. For example:

X argues for stricter gun control legislation, saying that the crime rate is on the rise and that we need to restrict the circulation of guns. I agree that the crime rate is on the rise, but that's precisely why I oppose stricter gun control legislation. We need to own guns to protect ourselves against criminals.

In this example of the "twist it" move, the writer agrees with X's claim that the crime rate is on the rise but then argues that this increasing crime rate is in fact a valid reason for *opposing* gun control legislation.

At times you might be reluctant to express disagreement, for any number of reasons—not wanting to be unpleasant, to hurt someone's feelings, or to make yourself vulnerable to being disagreed with in return. One of these reasons may in fact explain why the conference speaker we described at the start of Chapter 1 avoided mentioning the disagreement he had with other scholars until he was provoked to do so in the discussion that followed his talk.

As much as we understand such fears of conflict and have experienced them ourselves, we nevertheless believe it is better to state our disagreements in frank yet considerate ways than to deny them. After all, suppressing disagreements doesn't make them go away; it only pushes them underground, where they can fester in private unchecked. Nevertheless, disagreements do not need to take the form of personal put-downs. Furthermore, there is usually no reason to take issue with *every* aspect of someone else's views. You can single out for criticism only those aspects of what someone else has said that are troubling, and then agree with the rest—although such an approach, as we will see later in this chapter, leads to the somewhat more complicated terrain of both agreeing and disagreeing at the same time.

AGREE—BUT WITH A DIFFERENCE

Like disagreeing, agreeing is less simple than it may appear. Just as you need to avoid simply contradicting views you disagree with, you also need to do more than simply echo views you agree with. Even as you're agreeing, it's important to bring something new and fresh to the table, adding something that makes you a valuable participant in the conversation.

There are many moves that enable you to contribute something of your own to a conversation even as you agree with what someone else has said. You may point out some unnoticed evidence or line of reasoning that supports X's claims that X herself hadn't mentioned. You may cite some corroborating personal experience, or a situation not mentioned by X that her views help readers understand. If X's views are particularly challenging or esoteric, what you bring to the table could be an accessible translation—an explanation for readers not already in the know. In other words, your text can usefully contribute to the conversation simply by pointing out unnoticed implications or explaining something that needs to be better understood.

Whatever mode of agreement you choose, the important thing is to open up some difference or contrast between your position and the one you're agreeing with rather than simply parroting what it says.

TEMPLATES FOR AGREEING

▸ I agree that <u>diversity in the student body is educationally valuable</u> because my experience <u>at Central University</u> confirms it.

▸ X is surely right about _____ because, as she may not be aware, recent studies have shown that _____.

▸ X's theory of _____ is extremely useful because it sheds light on the difficult problem of _____.

▸ Those unfamiliar with this school of thought may be interested to know that it basically boils down to _____.

Some writers avoid the practice of agreeing almost as much as others avoid disagreeing. In a culture like America's that prizes originality, independence, and competitive individualism, writers sometimes don't like to admit that anyone else has made the same point, seemingly beating them to the punch. In our view, however, as long as you can support a view taken by someone else without merely restating what he or she has said, there is no reason to worry about being "unoriginal." Indeed, there is good reason to rejoice when you agree with others since those others can lend credibility to your argument. While you don't want to present yourself as a mere copycat of someone else's views, you also need to avoid sounding like a lone voice in the wilderness.

But do be aware that whenever you agree with one person's view, you are likely disagreeing with someone else's. It is hard to align yourself with one position without at least implicitly positioning yourself against others. The psychologist Carol Gilligan does just that in an essay in which she agrees with scientists who argue that the human brain is "hard-wired" for cooperation, but in so doing aligns herself against anyone who believes that the brain is wired for selfishness and competition.

> These findings join a growing convergence of evidence across the human sciences leading to a revolutionary shift in consciousness. . . . If cooperation, typically associated with altruism and self-sacrifice, sets off the same signals of delight as pleasures commonly associated with hedonism and self-indulgence; if the opposition between selfish and selfless, self vs. relationship biologically makes no sense, then a new paradigm is necessary to reframe the very terms of the conversation.
>
> CAROL GILLIGAN, "Sisterhood Is Pleasurable:
> A Quiet Revolution in Psychology"

In agreeing with some scientists that "the opposition between selfish and selfless . . . makes no sense," Gilligan implicitly disagrees with anyone who thinks the opposition *does* make sense. Basically, what Gilligan says could be boiled down to a template.

> ▸ I agree that _____, a point that needs emphasizing since so many people still believe _____ .

> ▸ If group X is right that _____, as I think they are, then we need to reassess the popular assumption that _____ .

What such templates allow you to do, then, is to agree with one view while challenging another—a move that leads into the domain of agreeing and disagreeing simultaneously.

AGREE AND DISAGREE SIMULTANEOUSLY

This last option is often our favorite way of responding. One thing we particularly like about agreeing and disagreeing simultaneously is that it helps us get beyond the kind of "is too" / "is not" exchanges that often characterize the disputes of young children and the more polarized shouting matches of talk radio and TV.

TEMPLATES FOR AGREEING
AND DISAGREEING SIMULTANEOUSLY

"Yes and no." "Yes, but . . . " "Although I agree up to a point, I still insist . . . " These are just some of the ways you can make your argument complicated and nuanced while maintaining a clear, reader-friendly framework. The parallel structure—"yes and no"; "on the one hand I agree, on the other I disagree"—enables readers to place your argument on that map of positions we spoke of earlier in this chapter while still keeping your argument sufficiently complex.

Another aspect we like about this option is that it can be tipped subtly toward agreement or disagreement, depending on where you lay your stress. If you want to stress the disagreement end of the spectrum, you would use a template like the one below.

▶ Although I agree with X up to a point, I cannot accept his overriding assumption that <u>religion is no longer</u> a major force today.

Conversely, if you want to stress your agreement more than your disagreement, you would use a template like this one.

▶ Although I disagree with much that X says, I fully endorse his final conclusion that _____.

The first template above might be called a "yes, but . . . " move, the second a "no, but . . . " move. Other versions include the following.

▶ Though I concede that _____, I still insist that _____.

▶ X is right that _____, but she seems on more dubious ground when she claims that _____.

▶ While X is probably wrong when she claims that _____, she is right that _____.

▶ Whereas X provides ample evidence that _____, Y and Z's research on _____ and _____ convinces me that _____ instead.

Another classic way to agree and disagree at the same time is to make what we call an "I'm of two minds" or a "mixed feelings" move.

▸ I'm of two minds about X's claim that _____. On the one hand, I agree that _____. On the other hand, I'm not sure if _____.

▸ My feelings on the issue are mixed. I do support X's position that _____, but I find Y's argument about _____ and Z's research on _____ to be equally persuasive.

This move can be especially useful if you are responding to new or particularly challenging work and are as yet unsure where you stand. It also lends itself well to the kind of speculative investigation in which you weigh a position's pros and cons rather than come out decisively either for or against. But again, as we suggest earlier, whether you are agreeing, disagreeing, or both agreeing and disagreeing, you need to be as clear as possible, and making a frank statement that you are ambivalent is one way to be clear.

IS BEING UNDECIDED OKAY?

Nevertheless, writers often have as many concerns about expressing ambivalence as they do about expressing disagreement or agreement. Some worry that by expressing ambivalence they will come across as evasive, wishy-washy, or unsure of themselves. Others worry that their ambivalence will end up confusing readers who require decisive clear-cut conclusions.

The truth is that in some cases these worries are legitimate. At times ambivalence can frustrate readers, leaving them with the feeling that you failed in your obligation to offer the guidance they expect from writers. At other times, however, acknowledging that a clear-cut resolution of an issue is impossible can demonstrate your sophistication as a writer. In an academic culture that values complex thought, forthrightly declaring that you have mixed feelings can be impressive, especially after having ruled out the one-dimensional positions on your issue taken by others in the conversation. Ultimately, then, how ambivalent you end up being comes down to a judgment call based on different readers' responses to your drafts, on your knowledge of your audience, and on the challenges of your particular argument and situation.

Exercises

1. Read one of the essays at the back of this book, identifying those places where the author agrees with others, disagrees, or both.

2. Write an essay responding in some way to the essay that you worked with in the preceding exercise. You'll want to summarize and/or quote some of the author's ideas and make clear whether you're agreeing, disagreeing, or both agreeing and disagreeing with what he or she says. Remember that there are templates in this book that can help you get started; see Chapters 1–3 for templates that will help you represent other people's ideas, and Chapter 4 for templates that will get you started with your response.

FIVE

"AND YET"

Distinguishing *What* You *Say* from *What* They *Say*

———⌐回⌐———

IF GOOD ACADEMIC WRITING involves putting yourself into dialogue with others, it is extremely important that readers be able to tell at every point when you are expressing your own view and when you are stating someone else's. This chapter takes up the problem of moving from what *they* say to what *you* say without confusing readers about who is saying what.

DETERMINE WHO IS SAYING WHAT IN THE TEXTS YOU READ

Before examining how to signal who is saying what in your own writing, let's look at how to recognize such signals when they appear in the texts you read—an especially important skill when it comes to the challenging works assigned in school. Frequently, when students have trouble understanding difficult texts, it is not just because the texts contain unfamiliar ideas or words, but because the texts rely on subtle clues to let readers know when a particular view should be attributed to the writer or to someone else. Especially with texts that present a true dialogue of perspectives, readers need to be alert to the often subtle markers that indicate whose voice the writer is speaking in.

Consider how the social critic and educator Gregory Mantsios uses these "voice markers," as they might be called, to distinguish the different perspectives in his essay on America's class inequalities.

> "We are all middle-class," or so it would seem. Our national consciousness, as shaped in large part by the media and our political leadership, provides us with a picture of ourselves as a nation of prosperity and opportunity with an ever expanding middle-class life-style. As a result, our class differences are muted and our collective character is homogenized.
>
> Yet class divisions are real and arguably the most significant factor in determining both our very being in the world and the nature of the society we live in.
>
> GREGORY MANTSIOS, "Rewards and Opportunities:
> The Politics and Economics of Class in the U.S."

Although Mantsios makes it look easy, he is actually making several sophisticated rhetorical moves here that help him distinguish the common view he opposes from his own position.

In the opening sentence, for instance, the phrase "or so it would seem" shows that Mantsios does not necessarily agree with the view he is describing, since writers normally don't present views they themselves hold as ones that only "seem" to be true. Mantsios also places this opening view in quotation marks to signal that it is not his own. He then further distances himself from the belief being summarized in the opening paragraph by attributing it to "our national consciousness, as shaped in large part by the media and our political leadership," and then further attributing to this "consciousness" a negative, undesirable "result": one in which "our class differences" get "muted" and "our collective character" gets "homogenized," stripped of its diversity and distinctness. Hence, even before Mantsios has declared his own position in the second paragraph, readers can get a pretty solid sense of where he probably stands.

Furthermore, the second paragraph opens with the word "yet," indicating that Mantsios is now shifting to his own view (as opposed to the common view he has thus far been describing). Even the parallelism he sets up between the first and second paragraphs—between the first paragraph's claim that class differences do not exist and the second paragraph's claim that they do—helps throw into sharp relief the differences between the two voices. Finally, Mantsios's use of a direct, authoritative, declarative tone in the second paragraph also suggests a switch in voice. Although he does not use the words "I say" or "I argue," he clearly identifies the view he holds by presenting it not as one that merely *seems* to be true or that *others tell us* is true, but as a view that *is* true or, as Mantsios puts it, "real."

Paying attention to these voice markers is an important aspect of reading comprehension. Readers who fail to notice these markers often take an author's summaries of what someone else believes to be an expression of what the author himself or herself believes. Thus when we teach Mantsios's essay, some students invariably come away thinking that the statement "we are all middle-class" is Mantsios's own position rather than the perspective he is opposing, failing to see that in writing these words Mantsios acts as a kind of ventriloquist, mimicking what others say rather than directly expressing what he himself is thinking.

To see how important such voice markers are, consider what the Mantsios passage looks like if we remove them.

We are all middle-class. . . . We are a nation of prosperity and opportunity with an ever expanding middle-class life-style. . . .

Class divisions are real and arguably the most significant factor in determining both our very being in the world and the nature of the society we live in.

In contrast to the careful delineation between voices in Mantsios's original text, this unmarked version leaves it hard to tell where his voice begins and the voices of others end. With the markers removed, readers cannot tell that "We are all middle-class" represents a view the author opposes, and that "Class divisions are real" represents what the author himself believes. Indeed, without the markers, especially the "Yet," readers might well miss the fact that the second paragraph's claim that "Class divisions are real" contradicts the first paragraph's claim that "We are all middle class."

TEMPLATES FOR SIGNALING WHO IS SAYING WHAT IN YOUR OWN WRITING

To avoid confusion in your own writing, make sure that at every point your readers can clearly tell who is saying what. To do so, you can use as voice-identifying devices many of the templates presented in previous chapters.

▸ Although X makes the best possible case for <u>universal, government-funded health care</u>, I <u>am not persuaded</u>.

▸ My view, however, contrary to what X has argued, is that _____.

▸ Adding to X's argument, I would point out that _____.

▸ According to both X and Y, _____.

▸ Politicians, X argues, should _____.

▸ Most athletes will tell you that _____.

BUT I'VE BEEN TOLD NOT TO USE "I"

Notice that the first three templates above use the first-person "I" or "we," as do many of the templates in this book, thereby contradicting the common advice about avoiding the first person in academic writing. Although you may have been told that the "I" word encourages subjective, self-indulgent opinions rather than well-grounded arguments, we believe that texts using "I" can be just as well supported—or just as self-indulgent—as those that don't. For us, well-supported arguments are grounded in persuasive reasons and evidence, not in the use or nonuse of any particular pronouns.

Furthermore, if you consistently avoid the first person in your writing, you will probably have trouble making the key move addressed in this chapter: differentiating your views from those of others, or even offering your own views in the first place. But don't just take our word for it. See for yourself how freely the first person is used by the writers quoted in this book, and by the writers assigned in your courses.

Nevertheless, certain occasions may warrant avoiding the first person and writing, for example, that "she is correct" instead of "I think that she is correct." Since it can be monotonous to read an unvarying series of "I" statements ("I believe . . . I think . . . I argue"), it is a good idea to mix first-person assertions with ones like the following.

▸ X is right that certain common patterns can be found in the communities.

▸ The evidence shows that _____ .

▸ X's assertion that _____ does not fit the facts.

▸ Anyone familiar with _____ should agree that _____ .

One might even follow Mantsios's lead, as in the following template.

▸ But _____ are real, and are arguably the most significant factor in _____ .

One the whole, however, academic writing today, even in the sciences and social sciences, makes use of the first person fairly liberally.

See pp. 206–13 for an example of how a physicist uses the first person.

ANOTHER TRICK FOR IDENTIFYING WHO IS SPEAKING

To alert readers about whose perspective you are describing at any given moment, you don't always have to use overt voice markers like "X argues" followed by a summary of the argument. Instead, you can alert readers about whose voice you're speaking in by *embedding* a reference to X's argument in your own sentences. Hence, instead of writing:

Liberals believe that cultural differences need to be respected. I have a problem with this view, however.

you might write:

I have a problem with *what liberals call cultural differences.*

There is a major problem with the liberal doctrine of *so-called cultural differences.*

You can also embed references to something you yourself have previously said. So instead of writing two cumbersome sentences like:

Earlier in this chapter we coined the term "voice markers." We would argue that such markers are extremely important for reading comprehension.

you might write:

We would argue that "voice markers," as we identified them earlier, are extremely important for reading comprehension.

Embedded references like these allow you to economize your train of thought and refer to other perspectives without any major interruption.

TEMPLATES FOR EMBEDDING VOICE MARKERS

▶ X overlooks what I consider an important point about <u>cultural differences</u>.

▸ My own view is that what X insists is a _____ is in fact a
  _____ .

▸ I wholeheartedly endorse what X calls _____ .

▸ These conclusions, which X discusses in _____ , add weight
  to the argument that _____ .

When writers fail to use voice-marking devices like the ones
discussed in this chapter, their summaries of others' views tend to
become confused with their own ideas—and vice versa. When
readers cannot tell if you are summarizing your own views or
endorsing a certain phrase or label, they have to stop and think:
"Wait. I thought the author disagreed with this claim. Has she
actually been asserting this view all along?" or "Hmmm, I thought
she would have objected to this kind of phrase. Is she actually
endorsing it?" Getting in the habit of using voice markers will
keep you from confusing your readers and help alert you to similar markers in the challenging texts you read.

Exercises

1. To see how one writer signals when she is asserting her own
   views and when she is summarizing those of someone else,
   read the following passage by the social historian Julie
   Charlip. As you do so, identify those spots where Charlip
   refers to the views of others and the signal phrases she uses
   to distinguish her views from theirs.

   Marx and Engels wrote: "Society as a whole is more and more splitting up into two great hostile camps, into two great classes directly
   facing each other—the bourgeoisie and the proletariat" (10). If

only that were true, things might be more simple. But in late twentieth-century America, it seems that society is splitting more and more into a plethora of class factions—the working class, the working poor, lower-middle class, upper-middle class, lower uppers, and upper uppers. I find myself not knowing what class I'm from.

In my days as a newspaper reporter, I once asked a sociology professor what he thought about the reported shrinking of the middle class. Oh, it's not the middle class that's disappearing, he said, but the working class. His definition: if you earn thirty thousand dollars a year working in an assembly plant, come home from work, open a beer and watch the game, you are working class; if you earn twenty thousand dollars a year as a school teacher, come home from work to a glass of white wine and PBS, you are middle class.

How do we define class? Is it an issue of values, lifestyle, taste? Is it the kind of work you do, your relationship to the means of production? Is it a matter of how much money you earn? Are we allowed to choose? In this land of supposed classlessness, where we don't have the tradition of English society to keep us in our places, how do we know where we really belong? The average American will tell you he or she is "middle class." I'm sure that's what my father would tell you. But I always felt that we were in some no man's land, suspended between classes, sharing similarities with some and recognizing sharp, exclusionary differences from others. What class do I come from? What class am I in now? As an historian, I seek the answers to these questions in the specificity of my past.

JULIE CHARLIP, "A Real Class Act: Searching
for Identity in the Classless Society"

2. Study a piece of your own writing to see how many perspectives you account for and how well you distinguish your

own voice from those you are summarizing. Consider the following questions:

a. How many perspectives do you engage?
b. What other perspectives might you include?
c. How do you distinguish your views from the other views you summarize?
d. Do you use clear voice-signaling phrases?
e. What options are available to you for clarifying who is saying what?
f. Which of these options are best suited for this particular text?

If you find that you do *not* include multiple views or clearly distinguish between your views and others', revise your text to do so.

SIX

"Skeptics May Object"

Planting a Naysayer in Your Text

———⌐◻⌐———

THE WRITER Jane Tompkins describes a pattern that repeats itself whenever she writes a book or an article. For the first couple of weeks when she sits down to write, things go relatively well. But then in the middle of the night, several weeks into the writing process, she'll wake up in a cold sweat, suddenly realizing that she has overlooked some major criticism that readers will surely make against her ideas. Her first thought, invariably, is that she will have to give up on the project, or that she will have to throw out what she's written thus far and start over. Then she realizes that "this moment of doubt and panic is where my text really begins." She then revises what she's written in a way that incorporates the criticisms she's anticipated, and her text becomes stronger and more interesting as a result.

This little story contains an important lesson for all writers, experienced and inexperienced alike. It suggests that even though most of us are upset at the idea of someone criticizing our work, such criticisms can actually work to our advantage. Although it's naturally tempting to ignore criticism of our ideas, doing so may in fact be a big mistake, since our writing improves when we not only listen to these objections but give them an explicit hearing in our writing. Indeed, no single device more quickly improves a piece of writing than planting a naysayer in the text—saying, for example, that "although some readers may object" to something in your argument, you "would reply that _____."

ANTICIPATE OBJECTIONS

But wait, you say. Isn't the advice to incorporate critical views a recipe for destroying your credibility and undermining your argument? Here you are, trying to say something that will hold up, and we want you to tell readers all the negative things someone might say against you?

Exactly. We *are* urging you to tell readers what others might say against you, but our point is that doing so will actually *enhance* your credibility, not undermine it. As we argue throughout this book, writing well does not mean piling up uncontroversial truths in a vacuum; it means engaging others in a dialogue or debate—not only by opening your text with a summary of what others *have* said, as we suggest in Chapter 1, but also by imagining what others *might* say against your argument as it unfolds. Once you see writing as an act of entering a conversation, you should also see how opposing arguments can work for you rather than against you.

Paradoxically, the more you give voice to your critics' objections, the more you tend to disarm those critics, especially if you go on to answer their objections in convincing ways. When you entertain a counterargument, you make a kind of preemptive strike, identifying problems with your argument before others can point them out for you. Furthermore, by entertaining counterarguments, you show respect for your readers, treating them not as gullible dupes who will believe anything you say but as independent, critical thinkers who are aware that your view is not the only one in town. In addition, by imagining what others might say against your claims, you come across as a generous, broad-minded person who is confident enough to open himself or herself to debate—like the writer in Figure 5.

Conversely, if you don't entertain counterarguments, you may very likely come across as closed-minded, as if you think your beliefs are beyond dispute. You might also leave important questions hanging and concerns about your arguments unaddressed. Finally, if you fail to plant a naysayer in your text, you may find that you have very little to say. Our own students often say that entertaining counterarguments makes it easier to generate enough text to meet their assignment's page-length requirements.

Planting a naysayer in your text is a relatively simple move, as you can see by looking at the following passage from a book by the writer Kim Chernin. Having spent some thirty pages complaining about the pressure on American women to lose weight and be thin, Chernin inserts a whole chapter entitled "The Skeptic," opening it as follows.

> At this point I would like to raise certain objections that have been inspired by the skeptic in me. She feels that I have been ignoring some of the most common assumptions we all make about our bodies and these she wishes to see addressed. For example: "You know perfectly well," she says to me, "that you feel better when you lose weight. You buy new clothes. You look at yourself more eagerly in the mirror. When someone invites you to a party you don't stop and ask yourself whether you want to go. You feel sexier. Admit it. You like yourself better."
>
> KIM CHERNIN, *The Obsession: Reflections on the Tyranny of Slenderness*

FIGURE 5

The remainder of Chernin's chapter consists of her answers to this inner skeptic. In the face of the skeptic's challenge to her book's central premise (that the pressure to diet seriously harms women's lives), Chernin responds neither by repressing the skeptic's critical voice nor by giving in to it and relinquishing her own position. Instead, she embraces that voice and writes it into her text. Note too that instead of dispatching this naysaying voice quickly, as many of us would be tempted to do, Chernin stays with it and devotes a full paragraph to it. By borrowing some of Chernin's language, we can come up with templates for entertaining virtually any objection.

TEMPLATES FOR ENTERTAINING OBJECTIONS

▶ At this point I would like to raise some objections that have been inspired by the skeptic in me. She feels that I have been ignoring the complexities of the situation.

▶ Yet some readers may challenge my view by insisting that _____.

▶ Of course, many will probably disagree on the grounds that _____.

Note that the objections in the above templates are attributed not to any specific person or group, but to "skeptics," "readers," or "many." This kind of nameless, faceless naysayer is perfectly appropriate in many cases. But the ideas that motivate arguments and objections often can—and, where possible, should—be ascribed to a specific ideology or school of thought (for example, liberals, Christian fundamentalists, neopragmatists) rather than to anonymous anybodies. In other words, naysayers can be labeled, and you can add precision and impact to your writing by identifying what those labels are.

TEMPLATES FOR NAMING YOUR NAYSAYERS

▸ Here many *feminists* would probably object that gender does influence language.

▸ But *social Darwinists* would certainly take issue with the argument that _____.

▸ *Biologists*, of course, may want to question whether _____.

▸ Nevertheless, both *followers and critics of Malcolm X* will probably suggest otherwise and argue that _____.

To be sure, some people dislike such labels and may even resent having labels applied to themselves. Some feel that labels put individuals in boxes, stereotyping them and glossing over what makes each of us unique. And it's true that labels can be used inappropriately, in ways that ignore individuality and promote stereotypes. But since the life of ideas, including many of our most private thoughts, is conducted through groups and types rather than solitary individuals, intellectual exchange requires labels to give definition and serve as a convenient shorthand. If you categorically reject all labels, you give up an important resource and even mislead readers by presenting yourself and others as having no connection to anyone else. You also miss an opportunity to generalize the importance and relevance of your work to some larger conversation. When you attribute a position you are summarizing to liberalism, say, or historical materialism, your argument is no longer just about your own solitary views but about the intersection of broad ideas and habits of mind that many readers may already have a stake in.

The way to minimize the problem of stereotyping, then, is not to categorically reject labels but to refine and qualify their use, as the following templates demonstrate.

▸ Although not all *Christians* think alike, some of them will probably dispute my claim that _____.

▸ *Non-native English speakers* are so diverse in their views that it's hard to generalize about them, but some are likely to object on the grounds that _____.

Another way to avoid needless stereotyping is to qualify labels carefully, substituting "pro bono lawyers" for "lawyers" in general, for example, or "quantitative sociologists" for all "social scientists," and so on.

Templates for Introducing Objections Informally

Objections can also be introduced in more informal ways. For instance, you can frame objections in the form of questions.

▸ But is my proposal realistic? What are the chances of its actually being adopted?

▸ Yet is it necessarily true that _____? Is it always the case, as I have been suggesting, that _____?

▸ However, does the evidence I've cited prove conclusively that _____?

You can also let your naysayer speak directly.

▸ "Impossible," some will say. "You must be reading the research selectively."

Moves like this allow you to cut directly to the skeptical voice itself, as the singer-songwriter Joe Jackson does in the following excerpt from a 2003 *New York Times* article complaining about the restrictions on public smoking in New York City bars and restaurants.

> I like a couple of cigarettes or a cigar with a drink, and like many other people, I only smoke in bars or nightclubs. Now I can't go to any of my old haunts. Bartenders who were friends have turned into cops, forcing me outside to shiver in the cold and curse under my breath. . . . It's no fun. Smokers are being demonized and victimized all out of proportion.
>
> "Get over it," say the anti-smokers. "You're the minority." I thought a great city was a place where all kinds of minorities could thrive. . . . "Smoking kills," they say. As an occasional smoker with otherwise healthy habits, I'll take my chances. Health consciousness is important, but so are pleasure and freedom of choice.
>
> JOE JACKSON, "Want to Smoke? Go to Hamburg"

Jackson could have begun his second paragraph, in which he shifts from his own voice to that of his imagined naysayer, more formally, as follows: "Of course anti-smokers will object that since we smokers are in the minority, we should simply stop complaining and quietly make the sacrifices we are being called on to make for the larger social good." Or

"Anti-smokers might insist, however, that the smoking minority should submit to the non-smoking majority." We think, though, that Jackson gets the job done in a far more lively way with the more colloquial form he chooses. Borrowing a standard move of playwrights and novelists, Jackson cuts directly to the objectors' view and then to his own retort, then back to the objectors' view and then to his own retort again, thereby creating a kind of dialogue or miniature play within his own text. This move works well for Jackson, but only because he uses quotation marks and other voice markers to make clear at every point whose voice he is in.

See Chapter 5 for more advice on using voice markers.

REPRESENT OBJECTIONS FAIRLY

Once you've decided to introduce a differing or opposing view into your writing, your work has only just begun, since you still need to represent and explain that view with fairness and generosity. Although it is tempting to give opposing views short shrift, to hurry past them, or even to mock them, doing so is usually counterproductive. When writers make the best case they can for their critics (playing Peter Elbow's "believing game"), they actually bolster their credibility with readers rather than undermine it. They make readers think, "This is a writer I can trust."

See pp. 31–32 for more on the believing game.

We recommend, then, that whenever you entertain objections in your writing, you stay with them for several sentences or even paragraphs and take them as seriously as possible. We also recommend that you read your summary of opposing views with an outsider's eye: put yourself in the shoes of someone who disagrees with you and ask if such a reader would recognize himself in your summary. Would that reader think you have taken his views seriously, as beliefs that reasonable people might hold? Or would he detect a mocking tone or an oversimplification of his views?

There will always be certain objections, to be sure, that you believe do not deserve to be represented, just as there will be objections that seem so unworthy of respect that they inspire ridicule. Remember, however, that if you do choose to mock a view that you oppose, you are likely to alienate those readers who don't already agree with you—likely the very readers you want to reach. Also be aware that in mocking another's view you may contribute to a hostile argument culture in which someone may ridicule you in return.

ANSWER OBJECTIONS

Do be aware that when you represent objections successfully, you still need to be able to answer those objections persuasively. After all, when you write objections into a text, you take the risk that readers will find those objections more convincing than the argument you yourself are advancing. In the editorial quoted above, for example, Joe Jackson takes the risk that readers will identify more with the anti-smoking view he summarizes than with the pro-smoking position he endorses.

This is precisely what Benjamin Franklin describes happening to himself in *The Autobiography of Benjamin Franklin* (1793), when he recalls being converted to Deism (a religion that exalts reason over spirituality) by reading *anti*-Deist books. When he encountered the views of Deists being negatively summarized by authors who opposed them, Franklin explains, he ended up finding the Deist position more persuasive. To avoid having this kind if unintentional reverse effect on readers, you need to do your best to make sure that any counterarguments you address are not more convincing than your own claims. It is good to address objections in your writing, but only if you are able to overcome them.

One surefire way to *fail* to overcome an objection is to dismiss it out of hand—saying, for example, "That's just wrong." The difference between such a response (which offers no supporting reasons whatsoever) and the types of nuanced responses we're promoting in this book is the difference between bullying your readers and genuinely persuading them.

Often the best way to overcome an objection is not to try to refute it completely but to agree with part of it while challenging only the part you dispute. In other words, in answering counterarguments, it is often best to say "yes, but" or "yes and no," treating the counterview as an opportunity to revise and refine your own position. Rather than build your argument into an impenetrable fortress, it is often best to make concessions while still standing your ground, as Kim Chernin does in the following response to the counterargument quoted above. While in the voice of the "skeptic," Chernin writes: "Admit it. You like yourself better when you've lost weight." In response, Chernin replies as follows.

See pp. 61–66 for more on agreeing, with a difference.

Can I deny these things? No woman who has managed to lose weight would wish to argue with this. Most people feel better about themselves when they become slender. And yet, upon reflection, it seems to me that there is something precarious about this well-being. After all, 98 percent of people who lose weight gain it back. Indeed, 90 percent of those who have dieted "successfully" gain back more than they ever lost. Then, of course, we can no longer bear to look at ourselves in the mirror.

In this way, Chernin shows how you can use a counterview to improve and refine your overall argument by making a concession. Even as she concedes that losing weight feels good in the short run, she argues that in the long run the weight always returns, making the dieter far more miserable.

TEMPLATES FOR MAKING CONCESSIONS WHILE STILL STANDING YOUR GROUND

▶ Although I grant that the book is poorly organized, I still maintain that it raises an important issue.

▶ Proponents of X are right to argue that _____. But they exaggerate when they claim that _____.

▶ While it is true that _____, it does not necessarily follow that _____.

▶ On the one hand, I agree with X that _____. But on the other hand, I still insist that _____.

Templates like these show that answering naysayers' objections does not have to be an all-or-nothing affair in which you either definitively refute your critics or they definitively refute you. Often the most productive engagements among differing views end with a combined vision that incorporates elements of each one.

But what if you've tried out all the possible answers you can think of to an objection you've anticipated and you *still* have a nagging feeling that the objection is more convincing than your argument itself? In that case, the best remedy is to go back and make some fundamental revisions to your argument, even reversing your position completely if need be. Although finding out late in the game that you aren't fully convinced by your own argument can be painful, it can actually make your final text more intellectually honest, challenging, and serious. After all, the goal of writing is not to keep proving that whatever you initially said is right, but to stretch the limits of your thinking. So if planting a strong naysayer in your text forces you to change your mind, that's not a bad thing. Some would argue that that is what the academic world is all about.

Exercises

1. Read the following passage by the cultural critic Eric Schlosser. As you'll see, he hasn't planted any naysayers in this text. Do it for him. Insert a brief paragraph stating an objection to his argument and then responding to the objection as he might.

   The United States must declare an end to the war on drugs. This war has filled the nation's prisons with poor drug addicts and small-time drug dealers. It has created a multibillion-dollar black market, enriched organized crime groups and promoted the corruption of government officials throughout the world. And it has not stemmed the widespread use of illegal drugs. By any rational measure, this war has been a total failure.

   We must develop public policies on substance abuse that are guided not by moral righteousness or political expediency but by common sense. The United States should immediately decriminalize the cultivation and possession of small amounts of marijuana for personal use. Marijuana should no longer be classified as a Schedule I narcotic, and those who seek to use marijuana as medicine should no longer face criminal sanctions. We must shift our entire approach to drug abuse from the criminal justice system to the public health system. Congress should appoint an independent commission to study the harm-reduction policies that have been adopted in Switzerland, Spain, Portugal, and the Netherlands. The commission should recommend policies for the United States based on one important criterion: what works.

In a nation where pharmaceutical companies advertise powerful antidepressants on billboards and where alcohol companies run amusing beer ads during the Super Bowl, the idea of a "drug-free society" is absurd. Like the rest of American society, our drug policy would greatly benefit from less punishment and more compassion.

ERIC SCHLOSSER, "A People's Democratic Platform"

2. Look over something you've written that makes an argument. Check to see if you've anticipated and responded to any objections. If not, revise your text to do so. If so, have you anticipated all the likely objections? Who if anyone have you attributed the objections to? Have you represented the objections fairly? Have you answered them well enough, or do you think you now need to qualify your own argument? Could you use any of the language suggested in this chapter? Does the introduction of a naysayer strengthen your argument? Why, or why not?

SEVEN

"So What? Who Cares?"

Saying Why It Matters

—❏—

BASEBALL IS the national pastime. Bernini was the best sculptor of the baroque period. All writing is conversational. So what? Who cares? Why does any of this matter?

How many times have you had reason to ask these questions? Regardless of how interesting a topic may be to you as a writer, readers always need to know what is at stake in a text and why they should care. All too often, however, these questions are left unanswered—mainly because writers and speakers assume that audiences will know the answers already or will figure them out on their own. As a result, students come away from lectures feeling like outsiders to what they've just heard, just as many of us feel left hanging after talks we've attended. The problem is not necessarily that the speakers lack a clear, well-focused thesis or that the thesis is inadequately supported with evidence. Instead, the problem is that the speakers don't address the crucial question of why their arguments matter.

That this question is so often left unaddressed is unfortunate since the speakers generally *could* offer interesting, engaging answers. When pressed, for instance, most academics will tell you that their lectures and articles matter because they address some belief that needs to be corrected or updated—and because their arguments have important, real-world consequences. Yet many academics fail to identify these reasons and consequences explicitly in what they say and write. Rather than assume that audiences will know why their claims matter, all writers need to answer the "so what?" and "who cares?" questions up front. Not everyone can claim to have a cure for cancer or a solution to end poverty. But writers who fail to show that others *should* care or already *do* care about their claims will ultimately lose their audiences' interest.

This chapter focuses on various moves that you can make to answer the "who cares?" and "so what?" questions in your own writing. In one sense, the two questions get at the same thing: the relevance or importance of what you are saying. Yet they get at this significance in different ways. Whereas "who cares?" literally asks you to identify a person or group who cares about your claims, "so what?" asks about the real-world applications and consequences of those claims—what difference it would make if they were accepted. We'll look first at ways of making clear who cares.

"WHO CARES?"

To see how one writer answers the "who cares?" question, consider the following passage from the science writer Denise Grady. Writing in the *New York Times*, she explains some of the latest research into fat cells.

> Scientists used to think body fat and the cells it was made of were pretty much inert, just an oily storage compartment. But within the past decade research has shown that fat cells act like chemical factories and that body fat is potent stuff: a highly active

tissue that secretes hormones and other substances with profound and sometimes harmful effects. . . .

In recent years, biologists have begun calling fat an "endocrine organ," comparing it to glands like the thyroid and pituitary, which also release hormones straight into the bloodstream.

DENISE GRADY, "The Secret Life of a Potent Cell"

Notice how Grady's writing reflects the central advice we give in this book, offering a clear claim and also framing that claim as a response to what someone else has said. In so doing, Grady immediately identifies at least one group with a stake in the new research that sees fat as "active," "potent stuff": namely, the scientific community, which formerly believed that body fat is inert. By referring to these scientists, Grady implicitly acknowledges that her text is part of a larger conversation and shows who besides herself has an interest in what she says.

Consider, however, how the passage would read had Grady left out what "scientists used to think" and simply explained the new findings in isolation.

> Within the past few decades research has shown that fat cells act like chemical factories and that body fat is potent stuff: a highly active tissue that secretes hormones and other substances. In recent years, biologists have begun calling fat an "endocrine organ," comparing it to glands like the thyroid and pituitary, which also release hormones straight into the bloodstream.

Though this statement is clear and easy to follow, it lacks any indication that anyone needs to hear it. Okay, one nods while reading this passage, fat is an active, potent thing. Sounds plausible enough; no reason to think it's not true. But does anyone really care? Who, if anyone, is interested?

TEMPLATES FOR INDICATING WHO CARES

To address "who cares?" questions in your own writing, we suggest using templates like the following, which echo Grady in refuting earlier thinking.

▸ Parents used to think <u>spanking was necessary</u>. But recently [or within the past few decades] experts suggest that <u>it can be counterproductive</u>.

▸ This interpretation challenges the work of those critics who have long assumed that _____.

▸ These findings challenge the work of earlier researchers, who tended to assume that _____.

▸ Recent studies like these shed new light on _____, which previous studies had not addressed.

Grady might have been more explicit by writing the "who cares?" question directly into her text, as in the following template.

▸ But who really cares? Who besides me and a handful of recent researchers has a stake in these claims? At the very least, the researchers who formerly believed _____ should care.

To gain greater authority as a writer, it can help to name specific people or groups who have a stake in your claims and to go into some detail about their views.

▸ Researchers have long assumed that _____. For instance, one eminent scholar of cell biology, _____, assumed in _____, her seminal work on cell structures and functions, that fat cells _____. As _____ herself put it, "_____" (2007). Another leading scientist, _____, argued that fat cells

" _____ " (2006). Ultimately, when it came to the nature of fat, the basic assumption was that _____ .

But a new body of research shows that fat cells are far more complex and that _____ .

In other cases, you might refer to certain people or groups who *should* care about your claims.

▸ If sports enthusiasts stopped to think about it, many of them might simply assume that the most successful athletes _____ . However, new research shows _____ .

▸ These findings challenge neoliberals' common assumption that _____ .

▸ At first glance, teenagers might say _____ . But on closer inspection _____ .

As these templates suggest, answering the "who cares?" question involves establishing the type of contrast between what others say and what you say that is central to this book. Ultimately, such templates help you create a dramatic tension or clash of views in your writing that readers will feel invested in and want to see resolved.

"So What?"

Although answering the "who cares?" question is crucial, in many cases it is not enough, especially if you are writing for general readers who don't necessarily have a strong investment in the particular clash of views you are setting up. In the case of Grady's argument about fat cells, such readers may still wonder why it matters that some researchers think fat cells are active, while others think they're inert. Or, to move to a different field of study, American literature, *so what* if some scholars disagree about Huck Finn's relationship with the runaway slave Jim in Mark Twain's *Adventures of Huckleberry Finn?* Why should anyone besides a few specialists in the field care about such disputes? What, if anything, hinges on them?

The best way to answer such questions about the larger consequences of your claims is to appeal to something that your audience already figures to care about. Whereas the "who cares?" question asks you to identify an interested person or group, the "so what?" question asks you to link your argument to some larger matter that readers already deem important. Thus in analyzing *Huckleberry Finn*, a writer could argue that seemingly narrow disputes about the hero's relationship with Jim actually shed light on whether Twain's canonical, widely read novel is a critique of racism in America or is itself marred by it.

Let's see how Grady invokes such broad, general concerns in her article on fat cells. Her first move is to link researchers' interest in fat cells to a general concern with obesity and health.

> Researchers trying to decipher the biology of fat cells hope to find new ways to help people get rid of excess fat or, at least, prevent obesity from destroying their health. In an increasingly obese world, their efforts have taken on added importance.

Further showing why readers should care, Grady's next move is to demonstrate the even broader relevance and urgency of her subject matter.

> Internationally, more than a billion people are overweight. Obesity and two illnesses linked to it, heart disease and high blood pressure, are on the World Health Organization's list of the top 10 global health risks. In the United States, 65 percent of adults weigh too much,

compared with about 56 percent a decade ago, and government researchers blame obesity for at least 300,000 deaths a year.

What Grady implicitly says here is "Look, dear reader, you may think that these questions about the nature of fat cells I've been pursuing have little to do with everyday life. In fact, however, these questions are extremely important—particularly in our 'increasingly obese world' in which we need to prevent obesity from destroying our health."

Notice that Grady's phrase "in an increasingly _____ world" can be adapted as a strategic move to address the "so what?" question in other fields as well. For example, a sociologist analyzing back-to-nature movements of the past thirty years might make the following statement.

> In a world increasingly dominated by cellphones and sophisticated computer technologies, these attempts to return to nature appear futile.

See p. 213 for an example from physics. This type of move can be readily applied to other disciplines because no matter how much disciplines may differ from one another, the need to justify the importance of one's concerns is common to them all.

Templates for Establishing Why Your Claims Matter

▸ *Huckleberry Finn* matters/is important because it is one of the most widely taught novels in the American school system.

▸ Although X may seem trivial, it is in fact crucial in terms of today's concern over _____ .

▸ Ultimately, what is at stake here is _____ .

▸ These findings have important implications for the broader domain of _____ .

▸ If we are right about _____ , then major consequences follow for _____ .

▸ These conclusions/This discovery will have significant applications in _____ as well as in _____ .

Finally, you can also treat the "so what?" question as a related aspect of the "who cares?" question.

▸ Although X may seem of concern to only a small group of _____ , it should in fact concern anyone who cares about _____ .

All these templates help you hook your readers. By suggesting the real-world applications of your claims, the templates not only demonstrate that others care about your claims but also tell your readers why *they* should care. Again, it bears repeating that simply stating and proving your thesis isn't enough. You also need to frame it in a way that helps readers care about it.

WHAT ABOUT READERS WHO ALREADY KNOW WHY IT MATTERS?

At this point, you might wonder if you need to answer the "who cares?" and "so what?" questions in *everything* you write. Is it really necessary to address these questions if you're proposing something so obviously consequential as, say, a treatment for autism or a program to eliminate illiteracy? Isn't it obvious that everyone cares about such problems? Does it really need to be spelled out? And what about when you're writing for audiences who you know are already interested in your claims and who understand perfectly well why they're important? In other words, do you always need to address the "so what?" and "who cares?" questions?

As a rule, yes—although it's true that you can't keep answering them forever and at a certain point must say enough is enough. Although a determined skeptic can infinitely ask why something matters—"Why should I care about earning a salary? And why should I care about supporting a family?"—you have to stop answering at some point in your text. Nevertheless, we urge you to go as far as possible in answering such questions. If you take it for granted that readers will somehow intuit the answers to "so what?" and "who cares?" on their own, you may make your work seem less interesting than it actually is, and you run the risk that readers will dismiss your text as irrelevant and unimportant. By conrast, when you are careful to explain who cares and why, it's a little like bringing a cheerleading squad into your text. And though some expert readers might already know why your claims matter, even they need to be reminded. Thus the safest move is to be as explicit as possible in answering the "so what?" question, even for those already in the know. When you step back from the text and explain why it matters, you are urging your audience to keep reading, pay attention, and care.

Exercises

1. Find several texts (scholarly pieces, newspaper articles, emails, memos, etc.) and see whether they answer the "so

what?" and "who cares?" questions. Probably some do, some don't. What difference does it make whether they do or do not? How do the authors who answer these questions do so? Do they use any strategies or techniques that you could borrow for your own writing? Are there any strategies or techniques recommended in this chapter, or that you've found or developed on your own, that you'd recommend to these authors?

2. Look over something you've written yourself. Do you indicate "so what?" and "who cares"? If not, revise your text to do so. You might use the following template to get started.

My point here (that _____) should interest those who _____. Beyond this limited audience, however, my point should speak to anyone who cares about the larger issue of _____.

3

TYING IT ALL TOGETHER

EIGHT

"As a Result"

Connecting the Parts

—◇—

WE ONCE HAD a student named Bill, whose characteristic sentence pattern went something like this.

> Spot is a good dog. He has fleas.

"Connect your sentences," we urged in the margins of Bill's papers. "What does Spot being good have to do with his fleas?" "These two statements seem unrelated. Can you connect them in some logical way?" When comments like these yielded no results, we tried inking in suggested connections for him.

> Spot is a good dog, *but* he has fleas.
> Spot is a good dog, *even though* he has fleas.

But our message failed to get across, and Bill's disconnected sentence pattern persisted to the end of the semester.

And yet Bill did focus well on his subjects. When he mentioned Spot the dog (or Plato, or any other topic) in one sentence, we could count on Spot (or Plato) being the topic of the following sentence as well. This was not the case with some of Bill's classmates, who sometimes changed topic from sentence to sentence or even from clause to clause within a single sentence. But because Bill neglected to mark his connections, his writing was as frustrating to read as theirs. In all these cases, we had to struggle to figure out on our own how the sentences and paragraphs connected or failed to connect with one another.

What makes such writers so hard to read, in other words, is that they never gesture back to what they have just said or forward to what they plan to say. "Never look back" might be their motto, almost as if they see writing as a process of thinking of something to say about a topic and writing it down, then thinking of something else to say about the topic and writing that down too, and on and on until they've filled the assigned number of pages and can hand the paper in. Each sentence basically starts a new thought, rather than growing out of or extending the thought of the previous sentence.

When Bill talked about his writing habits, he acknowledged that he never went back and read what he had written. Indeed, he told us that, other than using his computer software to check for spelling errors and make sure that his tenses were all aligned, he never actually reread what he wrote before turning it in. As Bill seemed to picture it, writing was something one did while sitting at a computer, whereas reading was a separate activity generally reserved for an easy chair, book in hand. It had never occurred to Bill that to write a good sentence he had to think about how it connected to those that came before and after; that he had to think hard about how that sentence fit into the sentences that surrounded it. Each sentence for Bill existed in a sort of tunnel isolated from every other sentence on the page. He never bothered to fit all the parts of his essay together because he apparently thought of writing as a matter of piling up information or observations rather than building a sustained argument. What we suggest in this chapter, then, is that you converse not only with others in your writing but with yourself: that you establish clear relations between one statement and the next by connecting those statements.

This chapter addresses the issue of how to connect all the parts of your writing. The best compositions establish a sense of momentum and direction by making explicit connections among their different parts, so that what is said in one sentence (or paragraph) both sets up what is to come and is clearly informed by what has already been said. When you write a sentence, you create an expectation in the reader's mind that the next sentence will in some way echo and extend it, even if—*especially if*—that next sentence takes your argument in a new direction.

It may help to think of each sentence you write as having arms that reach backward and forward, as Figure 6 suggests. When your sentences reach outward like this, they establish connections that help your writing flow smoothly in a way readers appreciate. Conversely, when writing lacks such connections and moves in fits and starts, readers repeatedly have to go back over the sentences and guess at the connections on their own. To prevent such disconnection and make your writing flow, we advise

FIGURE 6

following a "do it yourself" principle, which means that it is your job as a writer to do the hard work of making the connections rather than, as Bill did, leaving this work to your readers.

This chapter offers several strategies you can use to put this principle into action: (1) using transition terms (like "therefore" and "as a result"); (2) adding pointing words (like "this" or "such"); (3) developing a set of key terms and phrases for each text you write; and (4) repeating yourself, but with a difference—a move that involves repeating what you've said, but with enough variation to avoid being redundant. All these moves require that you always look back and, in crafting any one sentence, think hard about those that precede it.

Notice how we ourselves have used such connecting devices thus far in this chapter. The second paragraph of this chapter, for example, opens with the transitional "And yet," signaling a change in direction, while the opening sentence of the third includes the phrase "in other words," telling you to expect a restatement of a point we've just made. If you look through this book, you should be able to find many sentences that contain some word or phrase that explicitly hooks them back to something said earlier, to something about to be said, or both. And many sentences in *this* chapter repeat key terms related to the idea of connection: "connect," "disconnect," "link," "relate," "forward," and "backward."

Use Transitions

For readers to follow your train of thought, you need not only to connect your sentences and paragraphs to each other, but also to mark the kind of connection you are making. One of the easiest ways to make this move is to use *transitions* (from the Latin root *trans*, "across"), which help you cross from one point to another in your text. Transitions are usually placed at or near the start of sentences so they can signal to readers where your text is going: in the same direction it has been moving, or in a new direction. More specifically, transitions tell readers whether your text is echoing a previous sentence or paragraph ("in other words"), adding something to it ("in addition"), offering an example of it ("for example"), generalizing from it ("as a result"), or modifying it ("and yet").

The following is a list of commonly used transitions, categorized according to their different functions.

ADDITION

also	indeed
and	in fact
besides	moreover
furthermore	so too
in addition	

EXAMPLE

after all	specifically
as an illustration	to take a case in point
for example	consider
for instance	

ELABORATION

actually	to put it another way
by extension	to put it bluntly
in short	to put it succinctly
that is	ultimately
in other words	

COMPARISON

along the same lines	likewise
in the same way	similarly

CONTRAST

although	nevertheless
but	nonetheless
by contrast	on the contrary
conversely	on the other hand
despite	regardless
even though	whereas
however	while yet
in contrast	

CAUSE AND EFFECT

accordingly	so
as a result	then
consequently	therefore
hence	thus
since	

CONCESSION

admittedly	naturally
although it is true	of course
granted	to be sure

CONCLUSION

as a result	in sum
consequently	therefore
hence	thus
in conclusion	to sum up
in short	to summarize

Ideally, transitions should operate so unobtrusively in a piece of writing that they recede into the background and readers do not even notice that they are there. It's a bit like what happens when drivers use their turn signals before turning right or left: just as other drivers recognize such signals almost unconsciously, readers should process transition terms with a minimum of thought. But even though such terms should function unobtrusively in your writing, they can be among the most powerful tools in your vocabulary. Think how your heart sinks when someone, immediately after praising you, begins a sentence with "but" or "however." No matter what follows, you know it won't be good.

Notice that some transitions can help you not only to move from one sentence to another, but to combine two or more sentences into one. Combining sentences in this way helps prevent the choppy, staccato effect that arises when too many short sentences are strung together, one after the other. For instance, to combine Bill's two choppy sentences ("Spot is a good dog. He has fleas.") into one, better-flowing sentence, we suggested that he rewrite them as "Spot is a good dog, *even though* he has fleas."

Transitions like these not only guide readers through the twists and turns of your argument but also help ensure that you *have* an argument in the first place. In fact, we think of words like "but," "yet," "nevertheless," "besides," and others as argument words, since it's hard to use them without making some kind of argument. The word "therefore," for instance, commits you to making sure that the claims preceding it lead logically to the conclusion that it introduces. "For example" also assumes an argument, since it requires the material you are introducing to stand as an instance or proof of some preceding generalization. As a result, the more you use transitions, the more you'll be able not only to connect the parts of your text but also to construct a strong argument in the first place. And if you draw on them frequently enough, using them should eventually become second nature.

To be sure, it is possible to overuse transitions, so take time to read over your drafts carefully and eliminate any transitions that are unnecessary. But following the maxim that you need to learn the basic moves of argument before you can deliberately depart from them, we advise you not to forgo explicit transition terms until you've first mastered their use. In all our years of teaching, we've read countless essays that suffered from having few or no transitions, but cannot recall one in which the transitions were overused. Seasoned writers sometimes omit explicit transitions, but only because they rely heavily on the other types of connecting devices that we turn to in the rest of this chapter.

Before doing so, however, let us warn you about inserting transitions without really thinking through their meanings—using "therefore," say, when your text's logic actually requires "nevertheless" or "however." So beware. Choosing transition terms should involve a bit of mental sweat, since the whole point of using them is to make your writing *more* reader-friendly, not less. The only thing more frustrating than reading Bill-style passages like "Spot is a good dog. He has fleas" is reading misconnected sentences like "Spot is a good dog. For example, he has fleas."

Use Pointing Words

Another way to connect the parts of your argument is by using pointing words—which, as their name implies, point or refer backward to some concept in the previous sentence. The most common of these pointing words include "this," "these," "that," "those," "their," and "such" (as in "these pointing words" near the start of this sentence) and simple pronouns like "his," "he," "her," "she," "it," and "their." Such terms help you create the flow we spoke of earlier that enables readers to move effortlessly through your text. In a sense, these terms are like an invisible hand reaching out of your sentence, grabbing what's needed in the previous sentences and pulling it along.

Like transitions, however, pointing words need to be used carefully. It's dangerously easy to insert pointing words into your text that don't refer to a clearly defined object, assuming that because the object you have in mind is clear to you it will also be clear to your readers. For example, consider the use of "this" in the following passage.

> Alexis de Tocqueville was highly critical of democratic societies, which he saw as tending toward mob rule. At the same time, he accorded democratic societies grudging respect. *This* is seen in Tocqueville's statement that . . .

When "this" is used in such a way it becomes an ambiguous or free-floating pointer, since readers can't tell if it refers to Tocqueville's critical attitude toward democratic societies, his grudging respect for them, or some combination of both. "This what?" readers mutter as they go back over such passages and try to figure them out. It's also tempting to try to cheat with pointing words, hoping that they will conceal or make up for conceptual confusions that may lurk in your argument. By referring to a fuzzy idea as "this" or "that," you might hope the fuzziness will somehow come across as clearer than it is.

You can fix problems caused by a free-floating pointer by making sure there is one and only one possible object in the vicinity that the pointer could be referring to. It also often helps to name the object the pointer is referring to at the same time that you point to it, replacing the bald "this" in the example above with a more precise phrase like "this ambivalence toward democratic societies" or "this grudging respect."

REPEAT KEY TERMS AND PHRASES

A third strategy for connecting the parts of your argument is to develop a constellation of key terms and phrases, including their synonyms and antonyms, that you repeat throughout your text. When used effectively, your key terms should be items that readers could extract from your text in order to get a solid sense of your topic. Playing with key terms also can be a good way to come up with a title and appropriate section headings for your text.

Notice how often Martin Luther King Jr. uses the key words "criticism," "statement," "answer," and "correspondence" in the opening paragraph of his famous "Letter from Birmingham Jail."

Dear Fellow Clergymen:

While confined here in the Birmingham city jail, I came across your recent *statement* calling my present activities "unwise and untimely." Seldom do I pause to *answer criticism* of my work and ideas. If I sought to *answer* all the *criticisms* that cross my desk, my secretaries would have little time for anything other than *such correspondence* in the course of the day, and I would have no time for constructive work. But since I feel that you are men of genuine good will and that your *criticisms* are sincerely set forth, I want to try to *answer* your *statement* in what I hope will be patient and reasonable terms.

MARTIN LUTHER KING JR., *"Letter from Birmingham Jail"*

Even though King uses the terms "criticism" and "answer" three times each and "statement" twice, the effect is not overly repetitive. In fact, these key terms help build a sense of momentum in the paragraph and bind it together.

For another example of the effective use of key terms, consider the following passage, in which the historian Susan Douglas develops a constellation of sharply contrasting key terms around the concept of "cultural schizophrenics": women like herself who, Douglas claims, have mixed feelings about the images of ideal femininity with which they are constantly bombarded by the media.

> In a variety of ways, the mass media helped make us the cultural schizophrenics we are today, women who rebel against yet submit to prevailing images about what a desirable, worthwhile woman should be. . . . [T]he mass media has engendered in many women a kind of cultural identity crisis. We are ambivalent toward femininity on the one hand and feminism on the other. Pulled in opposite directions—told we were equal, yet told we were subordinate; told we could change history but told we were trapped by history—we got the bends at an early age, and we've never gotten rid of them.
>
> When I open *Vogue*, for example, I am simultaneously infuriated and seduced. . . . I adore the materialism; I despise the materialism. . . . I want to look beautiful; I think wanting to look beautiful is about the most dumb-ass goal you could have. The magazine stokes my desire; the magazine triggers my bile. And this doesn't only happen when I'm reading *Vogue*; it happens all the time. . . . On the one hand, on the other hand—that's not just me—that's what it means to be a woman in America.
>
> To explain this schizophrenia . . .
>
> Susan Douglas, Where the Girls Are:
Growing Up Female with the Mass Media

In this passage, Douglas establishes "schizophrenia" as a key concept and then echoes it through synonyms like "identity crisis," "ambivalent," "the bends"—and even demonstrates it through a series of contrasting words and phrases:

> rebel against / submit
> told we were equal / told we were subordinate
> told we could change history / told we were trapped by history
> infuriated / seduced
> I adore / I despise
> I want / I think wanting . . . is about the most dumb-ass goal
> stokes my desire / triggers my bile
> on the one hand / on the other hand

These contrasting phrases help flesh out Douglas's claim that women are being pulled in two directions at once. In so doing, they bind the passage together into a unified whole that, despite its complexity and sophistication, stays focused over its entire length.

Repeat Yourself—but with a Difference

The last technique we offer for connecting the parts of your text involves repeating yourself, but with a difference—which basically means saying the same thing you've just said, but in a slightly different way that avoids sounding monotonous. To effectively connect the parts of your argument and keep it moving forward, be careful not to leap from one idea to a different idea or introduce new ideas cold. Instead, try to build bridges between your ideas by echoing what you've just said while simultaneously moving your text into new territory.

Several of the connecting devices discussed in this chapter are ways of repeating yourself in this special way. Key terms, pointing terms, and even many transitions can be used in a way that not only brings something forward from the previous sentence but in some way alters it. When Douglas, for instance, uses the key term "ambivalent" to echo her earlier reference to schizophrenics, she is repeating herself with a difference—repeating the same concept, but with a different word that adds new associations.

In addition, when you use transition phrases like "in other words" and "to put it another way," you repeat yourself with a difference, since these phrases help you restate earlier claims but in a different register. When you open a sentence with "in other words," you are basically telling your readers that in case they didn't fully understand what you meant in the last sentence, you are now coming at it again from a slightly different angle, or that since you're presenting a very important idea, you're not going to skip over it quickly but will explore it further to make sure your readers grasp all its aspects.

We would even go so far as to suggest that after your first sentence, almost every sentence you write should refer back to previous statements in some way. Whether you are writing a "furthermore" comment that adds to what you have just said or a "for example" statement that illustrates it, each sentence should echo at least one element of the previous sentence in some discernible way. Even when your text changes direction and requires transitions like "in contrast," "however," or "but," you still need to mark that shift by linking the sentence to the one just before it, as in the following example.

> Cheyenne loved basketball. Nevertheless, she feared her height would put her at a disadvantage.

These sentences work because even though the second sentence changes course and qualifies the first, it still echoes key concepts from the first. Not only does "she" echo "Cheyenne," since both refer to the same person, but "feared" echoes "loved" by establishing the contrast mandated by the term "nevertheless." "Nevertheless," then, is not an excuse for changing subjects radically. It too requires repetition to help readers shift gears with you and follow your train of thought.

Repetition, in short, is the central means by which you can move from point A to point B in a text. To introduce one last analogy, think of the way experienced rock climbers move up a steep slope. Instead of jumping or lurching from one handhold to the next, good climbers get a secure handhold on the position they have established before reaching for the next ledge. The same thing applies to writing. To move smoothly from point to point in your argument, you need to firmly ground what you say in what you've already said. In this way, your writing remains focused while simultaneously moving forward.

"But hold on," you may be thinking. "Isn't repetition precisely what sophisticated writers should avoid, on the grounds that it will make their writing sound simplistic—as if they are belaboring the obvious?" Yes and no. On the one hand, writers certainly can run into trouble if they merely repeat themselves and nothing more. On the other hand, repetition is key to creating continuity in writing. It is impossible to stay on track in a piece of writing if you don't repeat your points throughout the length of the text. Furthermore, writers would never make an impact on readers if they didn't repeat their main points often enough to reinforce those points and make them stand out above subordinate points. The trick therefore is not to avoid repeating yourself but to repeat yourself in varied and interesting enough ways that you advance your argument without sounding tedious.

Exercises

1. Read the following opening to Chapter 2 of *The Road to Wigan Pier*, by George Orwell. Annotate the connecting devices by underlining the transitions, circling the key terms, and putting boxes around the pointing terms.

Our civilisation . . . is founded on coal, more completely than one realises until one stops to think about it. The machines that keep us alive, and the machines that make the machines, are all directly or indirectly dependent upon coal. In the metabolism of the Western world the coal-miner is second in importance only to the man who ploughs the soil. He is a sort of grimy caryatid upon whose shoulders nearly everything that is not grimy is supported. For this reason the actual process by which coal is extracted is well worth watching, if you get the chance and are willing to take the trouble.

When you go down a coal-mine it is important to try and get to the coal face when the "fillers" are at work. This is not easy, because when the mine is working visitors are a nuisance and are not encouraged, but if you go at any other time, it is possible to come away with a totally wrong impression. On a Sunday, for instance, a mine seems almost peaceful. The time to go there is when the machines are roaring and the air is black with coal dust, and when you can actually see what the miners have to do. At those times the place is like hell, or at any rate like my own mental picture of hell. Most of the things one imagines in hell are there—heat, noise, confusion, darkness, foul air, and, above all, unbearably cramped space. Everything except the fire, for there is no fire down there except the feeble beams of Davy lamps and electric torches which scarcely penetrate the clouds of coal dust.

When you have finally got there—and getting there is a job in itself: I will explain that in a moment—you crawl through the last line of pit props and see opposite you a shiny black wall three or four feet high. This is the coal face. Overhead is the smooth ceiling made by the rock from which the coal has been cut; underneath is the rock again, so that the gallery you are in is only as high as the ledge of coal itself, probably not much more than a yard. The first impression of all, overmastering everything else for a while, is the frightful, deafening din from the conveyor belt which carries the coal away. You cannot see very far, because the fog of coal dust throws back the beam of your lamp, but you can see on either side of you the line of half-naked kneeling men, one to every four or five yards, driving their shovels under the fallen coal and flinging it swiftly over their left shoulders . . . .

GEORGE ORWELL, *The Road to Wigan Pier*

2. Read over something you've written with an eye for the devices you've used to connect the parts. Underline all the transitions, pointing terms, key terms, and repetition. Do you see any patterns? Do you rely on certain devices more than others? Are there any passages that are hard to follow—and if so, can you make them easier to read by trying any of the other devices discussed in this chapter?

NINE

"AIN'T SO / IS NOT"

Academic Writing Doesn't Always Mean Setting Aside Your Own Voice

———⊡———

HAVE YOU EVER gotten the impression that writing well in college means setting aside the kind of language you use in everyday conversation? That to impress your instructors you need to use big words, long sentences, and complex sentence structures? If so, then we're here to tell you that it ain't necessarily so. On the contrary, academic writing can—and in our view *should*—be relaxed, easy to follow, and even a little bit fun. Although we don't want to suggest that you avoid using sophisticated, academic terms in your writing, we encourage you to draw upon the kinds of expressions and turns of phrase that you use every day when conversing with family and friends. In this chapter, we want to show you how you can write effective academic arguments while holding on to some of your own voice.

This point is important, since you may well become turned off from writing if you think your everyday language practices have to be checked at the classroom door. You may end up feeling like a student we know who, when asked how she felt about the writing she does in college, answered, "I do it because I have to, but it's just not me!"

This is not to suggest that *any* language you use among friends has a place in academic writing. Nor is it to suggest that you may fall back on colloquial usage as an excuse for not learning more rigorous forms of expression. After all, learning these more rigorous forms of expression and developing a more intellectual self is a major reason for getting an education. We do, however, wish to suggest that relaxed, colloquial language can often enliven academic writing and even enhance its rigor and precision. Such informal language also helps you connect with readers in a personal as well as an intellectual way. In our view, then, it is a mistake to assume that the academic and the everyday are completely separate languages that can never be used together.

Mix Academic and Colloquial Styles

Many successful writers blend academic, professional language with popular expressions and sayings. Consider, for instance, the following passage from a scholarly article about the way teachers respond to errors in student writing.

> Marking and judging formal and mechanical errors in student papers is one area in which composition studies seems to have a multiple-personality disorder. On the one hand, our mellow, student-centered, process-based selves tend to condemn marking formal errors at all. Doing it represents the Bad Old Days. Ms. Fidditch and Mr. Flutesnoot with sharpened red pencils, spilling innocent blood across the page. Useless detail work. Inhumane, perfectionist standards, making our students feel stupid, wrong,

trivial, misunderstood. Joseph Williams has pointed out how arbitrary and context-bound our judgments of formal error are. And certainly our noting of errors on student papers gives no one any great joy; as Peter Elbow says, English is most often associated *either* with grammar or with high literature—"two things designed to make folks feel most out of it."

Robert Connors and Andrea Lunsford,
"Frequency of Formal Errors in Current College Writing,
or Ma and Pa Kettle Do Research"

This passage blends writing styles in several ways. First, it places informal, relaxed expressions like "mellow," "the Bad Old Days," and "folks" alongside more formal, academic phrases like "multiple-personality disorder," "student-centered," "process-based," and "arbitrary and context-bound." Even the title of the piece, "Frequency of Formal Errors in Current College Writing, or Ma and Pa Kettle Do Research," blends formal, academic usage on the left side of the comma with a popular-culture reference to the fictional movie characters Ma and Pa Kettle on the right. Second, to give vivid, concrete form to their discussion of grading disciplinarians, Connors and Lunsford conjure up such archetypal, imaginary figures as the stuffy, old-fashioned taskmasters Ms. Fidditch and Mr. Flutesnoot. Through such imaginative uses of language, Connors and Lunsford inject greater force into what might otherwise have been dry, scholarly prose.

Formal/informal mixings like this can be found in countless other texts, though more frequently in the humanities than the sciences, and more frequently still in journalism. Notice how the food industry critic Eric Schlosser describes some changes in the city of Colorado Springs in his best-selling book on fast foods in the United States.

The loopiness once associated with Los Angeles has come full blown to Colorado Springs—the strange, creative energy that crops up where the future's consciously being made, where people walk the fine line separating a visionary from a total nutcase.

ERIC SCHLOSSER, *Fast Food Nation*

Schlosser could have played it safe and referred not to the "loopiness" but to the "eccentricity" associated with Los Angeles, or to "the fine line separating a visionary from a lunatic" instead of " . . . a total nutcase." His decision, however, to go with the more adventuresome, colorful terms gives a liveliness to his writing that would have been lacking with the more conventional terms.

Another example of writing that blends the informal with the formal comes from an essay on the American novelist Willa Cather by the literary critic Judith Fetterley. Discussing "how very successful Cather has been in controlling how we think about her," Fetterley, building on the work of another scholar, writes as follows.

As Merrill Skaggs has put it, "She is neurotically controlling and self-conscious about her work, but she knows at all points what she is doing. Above all else, she is self-conscious."

Without question, Cather was a control freak.

JUDITH FETTERLEY, "Willa Cather and the Question of Sympathy: The Unofficial Story"

This passage demonstrates not only that specialized phrases from psychology like "self-conscious" and "neurotically controlling" are compatible with everyday, popular expressions like "control freak," but also that translating the one type of language into the other, the specialized into the everyday, can help drive home a point. By translating Skaggs's polysyllabic description of Cather as "neurotically controlling and self-conscious" into the succinct, if blunt, claim that "Without question, Cather was a control freak," Fetterley suggests that one need not choose between rarified, academic ways of talking and the everyday language of casual conversation. Indeed, her passage offers a simple recipe for blending the high and the low: first make your point in the language of a professional field, and then make it again in everyday language— a great trick, we think, for underscoring a point.

See p. 198 for an essay that mixes colloquial and academic styles.

While one effect of blending languages like this is to give your writing more punch, another is to make a political statement—about the way, for example, society unfairly overvalues some dialects and devalues others. For instance, in the titles of two of her books, *Talkin and Testifyin: The Language of Black America* and *Black Talk: Words and Phrases from the Hood to the Amen Corner*, the language scholar Geneva Smitherman mixes African American vernacular phrases with more scholarly language in order to suggest, as she explicitly argues in these books, that black English vernacular is as legitimate a variety of language as "standard" English. Here are three typical passages.

In Black America, the oral tradition has served as a fundamental vehicle for gittin ovuh. That tradition preserves the Afro-American heritage and reflects the collective spirit of the race.

Blacks are quick to ridicule "educated fools," people who done gone to school and read all dem books and still don't know nothin!

. . . it is a socially approved verbal strategy for black rappers to talk about how bad they is.

—GENEVA SMITHERMAN, *Talkin and Testifyin:*
The Language of Black America

In these examples, Smitherman blends the standard written English of phrases like "oral tradition" and "fundamental vehicle" with black oral vernacular like "gittin ovuh," "dem books," and "how bad they is." Indeed, she even blends standard English spelling with that of black English variants like "dem" and "ovuh," thus mimicking what some black English vernacular actually sounds like. Although some scholars might object to these unconventional practices, this is precisely Smitherman's point: that our habitual language practices need to be opened up, and that the number of participants in the academic conversation needs to be expanded.

Along similar lines, the writer and activist Gloria Anzaldúa mixes standard English with Tex-Mex, a hybrid blend of English, Castilian Spanish, a North Mexican dialect, and the Indian language Nahuatl, to make a political point about the suppression of the Spanish language in the United States.

> From this racial, ideological, cultural, and biological cross-pollinization, an "alien" consciousness is presently in the making—a new *mestiza* consciousness, *una conciencia de mujer*.
>
> —Gloria Anzaldúa,
> *Borderlands / La Frontera: The New Mestiza*

Like Smitherman, Anzaldúa gets her point across not only through what she says but through the way she says it, literally showing that the new hybrid, or *mestiza*, consciousness that she describes is, as she puts it, "presently in the making." Ultimately, these passages suggest that blending languages— what Vershawn Ashanti Young calls "code meshing"—can call into question the very idea that the languages are distinct and separate.

WHEN TO MIX STYLES?
CONSIDER YOUR AUDIENCE AND PURPOSE

Because there are so many options in writing, you should never feel limited in your choice of words, as if such choices are set in stone. You can always experiment with your language and improve it. You can always dress it up, dress it down, or some combination of both. In dressing down your language, for example, you can make the claim that somebody "failed to notice" something by saying instead that it "flew under the radar." Or you can state that the person was "unaware" of something by saying that he was "out to lunch." You could even recast the title of this book, "*They Say / I Say,*" as a teenager might say it: "I'm Like / She Goes."

But how do you know when it is better to play things straight and stick to standard English, and when to be more adventuresome and mix things up? When, in other words, should you write "failed to notice" and when is it okay (or more effective) to write "flew under the radar"? Is it *always* appropriate to mix styles? And when you do so, how do you know when enough is enough?

In all situations, think carefully about your audience and purpose. When you write a letter applying for a job, for instance, or submit a grant proposal, where your words will be weighed by an official screening body, using language that's too colloquial or slangy may well jeopardize your chances of success. On such occasions, it is usually best to err on the safe side, conforming as closely as possible to the conventions of standard written English. In other situations for other audiences, however, there is room to be more creative—in this book, for example. Ultimately, your judgments about the appropriate language for the situation should always take into account your likely audience and your purpose in writing.

Although it may have been in the past, academic writing in most disciplines today is no longer the linguistic equivalent of a black-tie affair. To succeed as a writer in college, then, you need not always limit your language to the strictly formal. Although academic writing does rely on complex sentence patterns and on specialized, disciplinary vocabularies, it is surprising how often such writing draws on the languages of the street, popular culture, our ethnic communities, and home. It is by blending these languages that what counts as "standard" English changes over time and the range of possibilities open to academic writers continues to grow.

Exercises

1. Take a paragraph from this book and dress it down, rewriting it in informal colloquial language. Then rewrite the same paragraph again by dressing it up, making it much more formal. Then rewrite the paragraph one more time in a way that blends the two styles. Share your paragraphs with a classmate, and discuss which versions are most effective and why.

2. Find something you've written for a course, and study it to see whether you've used any of your own everyday expressions, any words or structures that are not "academic." If by chance you don't find any, see if there's a place or two where shifting into more casual or unexpected language would help you make a point, get your reader's attention, or just add liveliness to your text. Be sure to keep your audience and purpose in mind, and use language that will be appropriate to both.

TEN

"But Don't Get Me Wrong"

The Art of Metacommentary

—⟦⟧—

WHEN WE TELL PEOPLE that we are writing a chapter on the art of metacommentary, they often give us a puzzled look and tell us that they have no idea what "metacommentary" is. "We know what commentary is," they'll sometimes say, "but what does it mean when it's *meta*?" Our answer is that whether or not they know the term, they practice the art of metacommentary on a daily basis whenever they make a point of explaining something they've said or written: "What I meant to say was _____," "My point was not _____, but _____," or "You're probably not going to like what I'm about to say, but _____." In such cases, they are not offering new points but telling an audience how to interpret what they have already said or are about to say. In short, then, metacommentary is a way of commenting on your claims and telling others how—and how *not*—to think about them.

It may help to think of metacommentary as being like the chorus in a Greek play that stands to the side of the drama unfolding on the stage and explains its meaning to the audience—or like a voice-over narrator who comments on and explains the action in a television show or movie. Think of metacommentary as a sort of second text that stands alongside your main text and explains what it means. In the main text you say something; in the metatext you guide your readers in interpreting and processing what you've said.

What we are suggesting, then, is that you think of your text as two texts joined at the hip: a main text in which you make your argument and another in which you "work" your ideas, distinguishing your views from others they may be confused with, anticipating and answering objections, connecting one point to another, explaining why your claim might be controversial, and so forth. Figure 7 demonstrates what we mean.

THE MAIN TEXT SAYS SOMETHING, THE METATEXT TELLS READERS HOW — AND HOW NOT — TO THINK ABOUT IT.
FIGURE 7

Use Metacommentary to Clarify and Elaborate

But why do you need metacommentary to tell readers what you mean and guide them through your text? Can't you just clearly say what you mean up front? The answer is that, no matter how clear and precise your writing is, readers can still fail to understand it in any number of ways. Even the best writers can provoke reactions in readers that they didn't intend, and even good readers can get lost in a complicated argument or fail to see how one point connects with another. Readers may also fail to see what follows from your argument, or they may follow your reasoning and examples yet fail to see the larger conclusion you draw from them. They may fail to see your argument's overall significance, or mistake what you are saying for a related argument that they have heard before but that you want to distance yourself from. As a result, no matter how straightforward a writer you are, readers still need you to help them grasp what you really mean. Because the written word is prone to so much mischief and can be interpreted in so many different ways, we need metacommentary to keep misinterpretations and other communication misfires at bay.

Another reason to master the art of metacommentary is that it will help you develop your ideas and generate more text. If you have ever had trouble producing the required number of pages for a writing project, metacommentary can help you add both length and depth to your writing. We've seen many students who try to produce a five-page paper sputter to a halt at two or three pages, complaining they've said everything they can think of about their topic. "I've stated my thesis and presented my reasons and evidence," students have told us. "What else is there to do?" It's almost as if such writers have generated a thesis and don't know what to do with it. When these students learn to use metacommentary, however, they get more out of their ideas and write longer, more substantial texts. In sum, metacommentary can help you extract the full potential from your ideas, drawing out important implications, explaining ideas from different perspectives, and so forth.

So even when you may think you've said everything possible in an argument, try inserting the following types of metacommentary.

▸ In other words, she doesn't realize how right she is.

▸ What _____ really means is _____ .

▸ My point is not _____ but _____ .

▸ Ultimately, then, my goal is to demonstrate that _____ .

Ideally, such metacommentary should help you recognize some implications of your ideas that you didn't initially realize were there.

Let's look at how the cultural critic Neil Postman uses metacommentary in the following passage describing the shift he sees in American culture as it moves away from print and reading to television and movies.

> *It is my intention in this book to show* that a great . . . shift has taken place in America, with the result that the content of much of our public discourse has become dangerous nonsense. *With this in view, my task in the chapters ahead is* straightforward. *I must, first, demonstrate* how, under the governance of the printing press, discourse in America was different from what it is now—generally coherent, serious and rational; *and then* how, under the gov-

ernance of television, it has become shriveled and absurd. *But to avoid the possibility that my analysis will be interpreted as* standard-brand academic whimpering, a kind of elitist complaint against "junk" on television, *I must first explain that* . . . I appreciate junk as much as the next fellow, *and I know full well that* the printing press has generated enough of it to fill the Grand Canyon to over-flowing. Television is not old enough to have matched printing's output of junk.

NEIL POSTMAN, *Amusing Ourselves to Death:*
Public Discourse in the Age of Show Business

To see what we mean by metacommentary, look at the phrases above that we have italicized. With these moves, Postman essentially stands apart from his main ideas to help readers follow and understand what he is arguing.

He previews what he will argue: *It is my intention in this book to show* . . .

He spells out how he will make his argument: *With this in view, my task in these chapters . . . is. . . . I must, first, demonstrate . . . and then . . .*

He distinguishes his argument from other arguments it may easily be confused with: *But to avoid the possibility that my analysis will be interpreted as . . . I must first explain that . . .*

TITLES AS METACOMMENTARY

Even the title of Postman's book, *Amusing Ourselves to Death: Public Discourse in the Age of Show Business*, functions as a form of metacommentary since, like all titles, it stands apart from the text itself and tells readers the book's main point: that the very pleasure provided by contemporary show business is destructive.

Titles, in fact, are one of the most important forms of metacommentary, functioning rather like carnival barkers telling passersby what they can expect if they go inside. Subtitles, too, function as metacommentary, further explaining or elaborating on the main title. The subtitle of this book, for example, not only explains that it is about "the moves that matter in academic writing," but indicates that "they say / I say" is one of these moves. Thinking of a title as metacommentary can actually help you develop sharper titles, ones that, like Postman's, give readers a hint of what your argument will be. Contrast such titles with unhelpfully open-ended ones like "Shakespeare" or "Steroids" or "English Essay," or essays with no titles at all. Essays with vague titles (or no titles) send the message that the writer has simply not bothered to reflect on what he or she is saying and is uninterested in guiding or orienting readers.

Use Other Moves as Metacommentary

Many of the other moves covered in this book function as metacommentary: entertaining objections, adding transitions, framing quotations, answering "so what?" and "who cares?" When you entertain objections, you stand outside of your text and imagine what a critic might say; when you add transitions, you essentially explain the relationship between various claims. And when you answer the "so what?" and "who cares?" questions, you look beyond your central argument and explain who should be interested in it and why.

TEMPLATES FOR INTRODUCING METACOMMENTARY

TO WARD OFF POTENTIAL MISUNDERSTANDINGS

The following moves help you differentiate certain views from ones they might be mistaken for.

- ▶ Essentially, I am arguing not that <u>we should give up the policy</u>, but that <u>we should monitor effects far more closely</u>.

- ▶ This is not to say _____, but rather _____.

- ▶ X is concerned less with _____ than with _____.

TO ALERT READERS TO AN ELABORATION OF A PREVIOUS IDEA

The following moves elaborate on a previous point, saying to readers: "In case you didn't get it the first time, I'll try saying the same thing in a different way."

- ▶ In other words, _____.

- ▶ To put it another way, _____.

- ▶ What X is saying here is that _____.

TO PROVIDE READERS WITH A ROADMAP TO YOUR TEXT

This move orients readers, clarifying where you have been and where you are going—and making it easier for them to process and follow your text.

- ▶ Chapter 2 explores _____, while chapter 3 examines _____.

- ▶ Having just argued that _____, I want now to complicate the point by _____.

TEN   **"BUT DON'T GET ME WRONG"**

TO MOVE FROM A GENERAL CLAIM TO A SPECIFIC EXAMPLE

These moves help you explain a general point by providing a concrete example that illustrates what you're saying.

▸ For example, —————.

▸ —————, for instance, demonstrates —————.

▸ Consider —————, for example.

▸ To take a case in point, —————.

TO INDICATE THAT A CLAIM IS MORE, LESS, OR EQUALLY IMPORTANT

The following templates help you give relative emphasis to the claim that you are introducing, showing whether that claim is of more or less weight than the previous one, or equal to it.

▸ Even more important, —————.

▸ But above all, —————.

▸ Incidentally, we will briefly note, —————.

▸ Just as important, —————.

▸ Equally, —————.

▸ Finally, —————.

TO EXPLAIN A CLAIM WHEN YOU ANTICIPATE OBJECTIONS

Here's a template to help you anticipate and respond to possible objections.

▸ Although some readers may object that —————, I would answer that —————.

The Art of Metacommentary

These moves show that you are wrapping things up and tying up various subpoints previously made.

Chapter 6 has more templates for anticipating objections.

▶ In sum, then, _____.

▶ My conclusion, then, is that _____.

▶ In short, _____.

In this chapter we have tried to show that the most persuasive writing often doubles back and comments on its own claims in ways that help readers negotiate and process them. Instead of simply piling claim upon claim, effective writers are constantly "stage managing" how their claims will be recieved. It's true of course that to be persuasive a text has to have strong claims to argue in the first place. But even the strongest arguments will flounder unless writers use metacommentary to prevent potential misreadings and make their arguments shine.

Exercises

1. Read an essay or article and annotate it to indicate the different ways the author uses metacommentary. Use the templates on pp. 135–37 as your guide. For example, you may want to circle transitional phrases and write "trans" in the margins, to put brackets around sentences that elaborate on earlier sentences and mark them "elab," or underline sentences in which the author sums up what he or she has been saying, writing "sum" in the margins.

   How does the author use metacommentary? Does the author follow any of the templates provided in this book word for word? Did you find any forms of metacommentary not discussed in this chapter? If so, can you identify them, name them, and perhaps devise templates based on them for use in your own writing? And finally, how do you think the author's use of metacommentary enhances (or harms) his or her writing?

2. Complete each of the following metacommentary templates in any way that makes sense.

▸ In making a case for the medical use of marijuana, I am not saying that _____.

▸ But my argument will do more than prove that one particular industrial chemical has certain toxic properties. In this article, I will also _____.

▸ My point about the national obsessions with sports reinforces the belief held by many _____ that _____.

▸ I believe, therefore, that the war is completely unjustified. But let me back up and explain how I arrived at this conclusion: _____. In this way, I came to believe that this war is a big mistake.

4

IN SPECIFIC
ACADEMIC SETTINGS

ELEVEN

"I Take Your Point"

Entering Class Discussions

—⌐⌐—

Have you ever been in a class discussion that feels less like a genuine meeting of the minds than like a series of discrete, disconnected monologues? You make a comment, say, that seems provocative to you, but the classmate who speaks after you makes no reference to what you said, instead going off in an entirely different direction. Then, the classmate who speaks next makes no reference either to you or to any one else, making it seem as if everyone in the conversation is more interested in their own ideas than in actually conversing with anyone else.

We like to think that the principles this book advances can help improve class discussions, which increasingly include various forms of online communication. Particularly important for class discussion is the point that our own ideas become more cogent and powerful the more responsive we are to others, and the more we frame our claims not in isolation but as responses to what others before us have said. Ultimately, then, a good face-to-face classroom discussion (or online communication) doesn't just happen spontaneously. It requires the same sorts of disciplined moves and practices used in many writing situations, particularly that of identifying to what and to whom you are responding.

FRAME YOUR COMMENTS AS A RESPONSE
TO SOMETHING THAT HAS ALREADY BEEN SAID

The single most important thing you need to do when joining a class discussion is to link what you are about to say to something that has already been said.

▶ I really liked Aaron's point about the two sides being closer than they seem. I'd add that both seem rather moderate.

▶ I take your point, Nadia, that _____ . Still . . .

▶ Though Sheila and Ryan seem to be at odds about _____ , they may actually not be all that far apart.

In framing your comments this way, it is usually best to name both the person and the idea you're responding to. If you name the person alone ("I agree with Aaron because _____ "), it may not be clear to listeners what part of what Aaron said you are referring to. Conversely, if you only summarize what Aaron said without naming him, you'll probably leave your classmates wondering whose comments you're referring to.

But won't you sound stilted and deeply redundant in class if you try to restate the point your classmate just made? After all, in the case of the first template above, the entire class will have just heard Aaron's point about the two sides being closer than they seem. Why then would you need to restate it?

We agree that in oral situations, it does often sound artificial to restate what others just said precisely because they just said it. It would be awkward if, on being asked to pass the salt at lunch, one were to reply: "If I understand you correctly, you have asked me to pass the salt. Yes, I can, and here it is." But in oral discussions about complicated issues that are open to multiple interpretations, we usually do need to resummarize what others have said to make sure that everyone is on the same page. Since Aaron may have made several points when he spoke and may have been followed by other commentators, the class will probably need you to summarize which point of his you are referring to. And even if Aaron made only one point, restating that point is helpful, not only to remind the group what his point was (since some may have missed or forgotten it) but also to make sure that he, you, and others have interpreted his point in the same way.

To Change the Subject, Indicate Explicitly That You Are Doing So

It is fine to try to change the conversation's direction. There's just one catch: you need to make clear to listeners that this is what you are doing. For example:

▶ So far we have been talking about <u>the characters</u> in the <u>film</u>. But isn't the real issue here <u>the cinematography</u>?

▶ I'd like to change the subject to one that hasn't yet been addressed.

You can try to change the subject without indicating that you are doing so. But you risk that your comment will come across as irrelevant rather than as a thoughtful contribution that moves the conversation forward.

Be Even More Explicit
Than You Would Be in Writing

Because listeners in an oral discussion can't go back and reread what you just said, they are more easily overloaded than are readers of a print text. For this reason, in a class discussion you will do well to take some extra steps to help listeners follow your train of thought. (1) When you make a comment, limit yourself to one point only though you can elaborate on this point, fleshing it out with examples and evidence. If you feel you must make two points, either unite them under one larger umbrella point, or make one point first and save the other for later. Trying to bundle two or more claims into one comment can result in neither getting the attention it deserves. (2) Use metacommentary to highlight your key point so that listeners can readily grasp it.

▸ In other words, what I'm trying to get at here is _____.

▸ My point is this: _____.

▸ My point, though, is not _____, but _____.

▸ This distinction is important because _____.

TWELVE

"WHAT'S MOTIVATING THIS WRITER?"

Reading for the Conversation

—⊡—

"**W**HAT IS THE AUTHOR'S ARGUMENT? What is he or she trying to say?" For many years, these were the first questions we would ask our classes in a discussion of an assigned reading. The discussion that resulted was often halting, as our students struggled to get a handle on the argument, but eventually, after some awkward silences, the class would come up with something we could all agree was an accurate summary of the author's main thesis. Even after we'd gotten over that hurdle, however, the discussion would often still seem forced, and would limp along as we all struggled with the question that naturally arose next: Now that we had determined what the author was saying, what did we ourselves have to say?

For a long time we didn't worry much about these halting discussions, justifying them to ourselves as the predictable result of assigning difficult, challenging readings. Several years ago, however, as we started writing this book and began thinking about writing as the art of entering conversations, we latched onto the idea of leading with some different questions: "What other argument(s) is the writer responding to?" "Is the writer disagreeing or agreeing with something, and if so what?" "What is motivating the writer's argument?" "Are there other ideas that you have encountered in this class or elsewhere that might be pertinent?" The results were often striking. The discussions that followed tended to be far livelier and to draw in a greater number of students. We were still asking students to look for the main argument, but we were now asking them to see that argument as a response to some other argument that provoked it, gave it a reason for being, and helped all of us see why we should care about it.

What had happened, we realized, was that by changing the opening question, we changed the way our students approached reading, and perhaps the way they thought about academic work in general. Instead of thinking of the argument of a text as an isolated entity, they now thought of that argument as one that responded to and provoked other arguments. Since they were now dealing not with *one* argument but at least *two* (the author's argument and the one[s] he or she was responding to), they now had alternative ways of seeing the topic at hand. This meant that, instead of just trying to understand the view presented by the author, they were more able to question that view intelligently and engage in the type of discussion and debate that is the hallmark of a college education. In our discussions, animated debates often arose between students who found the author's argument convincing and others who were more convinced by the view it was challenging. In the best of these debates, the binary positions would be questioned by other students, who suggested each was too simple, that both might be right or that a third alternative was possible. Still other students might object that the discussion thus far had missed the author's real point and suggest that we all go back to the text and pay closer attention to what it actually said.

We eventually realized that the move from reading for the author's argument in isolation to reading for how the author's argument is in conversation with the arguments of others helps readers become active, critical readers rather than passive recipients of knowledge. On some level, reading for the conversation is more rigorous and demanding than reading for what one author says. It asks that you determine not only what the author thinks, but how what the author thinks fits with what others think, and ultimately with what you yourself think. Yet on another level, reading this way is a lot simpler and more familiar than reading for the thesis alone, since it returns writing to the familiar, everyday act of communicating with other people about real issues.

DECIPHERING THE CONVERSATION

We suggest, then, that when assigned a reading, you imagine the author not as sitting alone in an empty room hunched over a desk or staring at a screen, but as sitting in a crowded coffee shop talking to others who are making claims that he or she is engaging with. In other words, imagine the author as participating in an ongoing, multisided, conversation in which everyone is trying to persuade others to agree or at least to take his or her position seriously.

The trick in reading for the conversation is to figure out *what views the author is responding to* and *what the author's own argument is*—or, to put it in the terms used in this book, to determine the "they say" and how the author responds to it. One of the challenges in reading for the "they say" and "I say" can be figuring out which is which, since it may not be obvious when writers are summarizing others and when they are speaking for themselves. Readers need to be alert for any changes in voice that a writer might make, since instead of using explicit road-mapping phrases like "although many believe," authors may simply summarize the view that they want to engage with and indicate only subtly that it is not their own.

Consider again the opening to the selection by David Zinczenko on p. 195.

> If ever there were a newspaper headline custom made for Jay Leno's monologue, this was it. Kids taking on McDonald's this week, suing the company for making them fat. Isn't that like middle-aged men suing Porsche for making them get speeding tickets? Whatever happened to personal responsibility?
>
> I tend to sympathize with these portly fast-food patrons, though. Maybe that's because I used to be one of them.
>
> —David Zinczenko, "Don't Blame the Eater"

Whenever we teach this passage, some students inevitably assume that Zinczenko must be espousing the view expressed in his first paragraph: that suing McDonald's is ridiculous. When their reading is challenged by their classmates, these students point to the page and reply, "Look. It's right here on the page. This is what Zinczenko wrote. These are his exact words." The assumption these students are making is that if something appears on the page, the author must endorse it. In fact, however, we ventriloquize views that we don't believe in, and may in fact passionately disagree with, all the time. The central clues that Zinczenko disagrees with the view expressed in his opening

See Chapter 6 for more discussion of naysayers.

paragraph come in the second paragraph, when he finally offers a first-person declaration and uses a constrastive transition, "though," thereby resolving any questions about where he stands.

WHEN THE "THEY SAY" IS UNSTATED

Another challenge can be identifying the "they say" when it is not explicitly identified. Whereas Zinczenko offers an up-front summary of the view he is responding to, other writers assume that their readers are so familiar with these views that they need not name or summarize them. In such cases, you the reader have to reconstruct the unstated "they say" that is motivating the text through a process of inference.

See, for instance, if you can reconstruct the position that Tamara Draut is challenging in the opening paragraph of her essay "The Growing College Gap."

> "The first in her family to graduate from college." How many times have we heard that phrase, or one like it, used to describe a successful American with a modest background? In today's United States, a four-year degree has become the all-but-official ticket to middle-class security. But if your parents don't have much money or higher education in their own right, the road to college—and beyond—looks increasingly treacherous. Despite a sharp increase in the proportion of high school graduates going on to some form of postsecondary education, socio-economic status continues to exert a powerful influence on college admission and completion; in fact, gaps in enrollment by class and race, after declining in the 1960s and 1970s, are once again as wide as they were thirty years ago, and getting wider, even as college has become far more crucial to lifetime fortunes.
>
> —TAMARA DRAUT, "The Growing College Gap"

You might think that the "they say" here is embedded in the third sentence: They say (or we all think) that a four-year degree is "the all-but-official ticket to middle-class security," and you might assume that Draut will go on to disagree.

If you read the passage this way, however, you would be mistaken. Draut is not questioning whether a college degree has become "the ticket to middle-class security," but whether most Americans can obtain that ticket, whether college is within the financial reach of most American families. You may have been thrown off by the "but" following the statement that college has become a prerequisite for middle-class security. However, unlike the "though" in Zinczenko's opening, this "but" does not signal that Draut will be disagreeing with the view she has just summarized, a view that in fact she takes as a given. What Draut disagrees with is that this ticket to middle-class security is still readily available to the middle and working classes.

Were one to imagine Draut in a room talking with others with strong views on this topic, one would need to picture her challenging not those who think college is a ticket to financial security (something she agrees with and takes for granted), but those who think the doors of college are open to anyone willing to put forth the effort to walk through them. The view that Draut is challenging, then, is not summarized in her opening. Instead, she assumes that readers are already so familiar with this view that it need not be stated.

Draut's example suggests that in texts where the central "they say" is not immediately identified, you have to construct it yourself based on the clues the text provides. You have to start by locating the writer's thesis and then imagine some of the arguments that might be made against it. What would it look like to disagree with this view? In Draut's case, it is relatively easy to construct a counterargument: it is the familiar faith in the American Dream of equal opportunity when it comes to access to college. Figuring out the counterargument not only reveals what motivated Draut as a writer but helps you respond to her essay as an active, critical reader. Constructing this counterargument can also help you recognize how Draut challenges your own views, questioning opinions that you previously took for granted.

WHEN THE "THEY SAY" IS ABOUT SOMETHING "NOBODY HAS TALKED ABOUT"

Another challenge in reading for the conversation is that writers sometimes build their arguments by responding to a *lack* of discussion. These writers build their case not by playing off views that can be identified (like faith in the American Dream or the idea that we are responsible for our body weight), but by pointing to something others have overlooked. As the writing theorists John M. Swales and Christine B. Feak point out, one effective way to "create a research space" and "establish a niche" in the academic world is "by indicating a gap in . . . previous research." Much research in the sciences and humanities takes this "Nobody has noticed X" form.

In such cases, the writer may be responding to scientists, for example, who have overlooked an obscure plant that offers insights into global warming, or to literary critics who have been so busy focusing on the lead character in a play that they have overlooked something important about the minor characters.

READING PARTICULARLY CHALLENGING TEXTS

Sometimes it is difficult to figure out the views that writers are responding to not because these writers do not identify those views but because their language and the concepts they are dealing with are particularly challenging. Consider, for instance, the first two sentences of *Gender Trouble: Feminism and the Subversion of Identity*, a book by the feminist philosopher and literary theorist Judith Butler, thought by many to be a particularly difficult academic writer.

> Contemporary feminist debates over the meaning of gender lead time and again to a certain sense of trouble, as if the indeterminacy of gender might eventually culminate in the failure of feminism. Perhaps trouble need not carry such a negative valence.
>
> —Judith Butler, *Gender Trouble: Feminism and the Subversion of Identity*

There are many reasons readers may stumble over this relatively short passage, not the least of which is that Butler does not explicitly indicate where her own view begins and the view she is responding to ends. Unlike Zinczenko, Butler does not use the first-person "I" or a phrase such as "in my own view" to show that the position in the second sentence is her own. Nor does Butler offer a clear transition such as "but" or "however" at the start of the second sentence to indicate, as Zinczenko does with "though," that in the second sentence she is questioning the argument she has summarized in the first. And finally, like many academic writers, Butler uses abstract, unfamiliar words that many readers may need to look up, like "gender" (sexual identity, male or female), "indeterminacy" (the quality of being impossible to define or pin down), "culminate" (finally result in), and "negative valence" (a term borrowed from chemistry, roughly denoting "negative significance" or "meaning"). For all these reasons, we can imagine many readers feeling intimidated before they reach the third sentence of Butler's book.

But readers who break down this passage into its essential parts will find that it is actually a lucid piece of writing that conforms to the classic "they say / I say" pattern. Though it can be difficult to spot the clashing arguments in the two sentences, close analysis reveals that the first sentence offers a way of looking at a certain type of "trouble" in the realm of feminist politics that is being challenged in the second.

To understand difficult passages of this kind, you need to translate them into your own words—to build a bridge, in effect, between the passage's unfamiliar terms and ones more familiar to you. Building such a bridge should help you connect what you already know to what the author is saying—and will then help you move from reading to writing, providing you with some of the language you will need to summarize the text. One major challenge in translating the author's words into your own, however, is to stay true to what the author is actually saying, avoiding what we call "the closest cliché syndrome," in which one mistakes a commonplace idea for an author's more complex one (mistaking Butler's critique of the concept of "woman," for instance, for the common idea that women must have equal rights). The work of complex writers like Butler, who frequently challenge conventional thinking, cannot always be collapsed into the types of ideas most of us are already familiar with. Therefore, when you translate, do not try to fit the ideas of such writers into your preexisting beliefs, but instead allow your own views to be challenged. In building a bridge to the writers you read, it is often necessary to meet those writers more than halfway.

For more on the closest cliché syndrome, see Chapter 2.

So what, then, does Butler's opening say? Translating Butler's words into terms that are easier to understand, we can see that the first sentence says that for many feminists today, "the indeterminacy of gender"—the inability to define the essence of sexual identity—spells the end of feminism; that for many feminists the inability to define "gender," presumably the building block of the feminist movement, means serious "trouble" for feminist politics. In contrast, the second sentence suggests that this same "trouble" need not be thought of in such "negative" terms, that the inability to define femininity, or "gender trouble" as Butler calls it in her book's title, may not be such a bad thing—and, as she goes on to argue in the pages that follow, may even be something that feminist activists can profit from. In other words, Butler suggests, highlighting uncertainties about masculinity and femininity can be a powerful feminist tool.

Pulling all these inferences together, then, the opening sentences can be translated as follows: "While many contemporary feminists believe that uncertainty about what it means to be a woman will undermine feminist politics, I, Judith Butler, believe that this uncertainty can actually help strengthen feminist politics." Translating Butler's point into our own book's basic move: "They say that if we cannot define 'woman,' feminism is in big trouble. But I say that this type of trouble is precisely what feminism needs." Despite its difficulty, then, we hope you agree that this initially intimidating passage does make sense if you stay with it.

We hope it is clear that critical reading is a two-way street. It is just as much about being open to the way that writers can challenge you, maybe even transform you, as it is about questioning those writers. And if you translate a writer's argument into your own words as you read, you should allow the text to take you outside the ideas that you already hold and to introduce you to new terms and concepts. Even if you end up disagreeing with an author, you first have to show that you have really listened to what he or she is saying, have fully grasped his or her arguments, and can accurately summarize those arguments. Without such deep, attentive listening, any critique you make will be superficial and decidedly *uncritical*. It will be a critique that says more about you than about the writer or idea you're supposedly responding to.

In this chapter we have tried to show that reading for the conversation means looking not just for the thesis of a text in isolation but for the view or views that motivate that thesis—the "they say." We have also tried to show that reading for the conversation means being alert for the different strategies writers use to engage the view(s) that are motivating them, since not all writers engage other perspectives in the same way. Some writers explicitly identify and summarize a view they are responding to at the outset of their text and then return to it frequently as their text unfolds. Some refer only obliquely to a view that is motivating them, assuming that readers will be able to reconstruct that view on their own. Other writers may not explicitly distinguish their own view from the views they are questioning in ways that all of us find clear, leaving some readers to wonder whether a given view is the writer's own or one that he or she is challenging. And some writers push off against the "they say" that is motivating them in a challenging academic language that requires readers to translate what they are saying into more accessible, everyday terms. In sum, then, though most persuasive writers do follow a conversational "they say / I say" pattern, they do so in a great variety of ways. What this means for readers is that they need to be armed with various strategies for detecting the conversations in what they read, even when those conversations are not self-evident.

THIRTEEN

"THE DATA SUGGEST"

Writing in the Sciences

CHRISTOPHER GILLEN

———

CHARLES DARWIN DESCRIBED *On the Origin of Species* as "one long argument." In *Dialogue Concerning the Two Chief World Systems*, Galileo Galilei cast his argument for a sun-centered solar system as a series of conversations. As these historical examples show, scientific writing is fundamentally argumentative. Like all academic writers, scientists make and defend claims. They address disagreements and explore unanswered questions. They propose novel mechanisms and new theories. And they advance certain explanations and reject others. Though their vocabulary may be more technical and their emphasis more numerical, science writers use the same

CHRISTOPHER GILLEN is a professor of biology at Kenyon College. He teaches comparative animal physiology, integrative animal biology, and biology of exercise as well as introductory lecture and lab classes in biology. One focus of his teaching is helping students critically read primary research articles.

rhetorical moves as other academic writers. Consider the following example from a 2006 book about the laws of physics.

> The common refrain that is heard in elementary discussions of quantum mechanics is that a physical object is in some sense both a wave and a particle, with its wave nature apparent when you measure a wave property such as wavelength, and its particle nature apparent when you measure a particle property such as position. But this is, at best, misleading and, at worst, wrong.
>
> V. J. STENGER, *The Comprehensible Cosmos*, 2006

The "they say / I say" structure of this passage is unmistakable: They say that objects have properties of both waves and particles; I say they are wrong. This example is not a lonely argumentative passage cherry-picked from an otherwise nonargumentative text. Rather, Stenger's entire book makes the argument that is foreshadowed by its title, *The Comprehensible Cosmos*: that although some might see the universe as hopelessly complex, it is essentially understandable.

Here's another argumentative passage, this one from a 2001 research article about the role of lactic acid in muscle fatigue:

> In contrast to the often suggested role for acidosis as a cause of muscle fatigue, it is shown that in muscles where force was depressed by high $[K^+]_o$, acidification by lactic acid produced a pronounced recovery of force.
>
> O. B. NIELSEN, F. DE PAOLI, AND K. OVERGAARD, "Protective Effects of Lactic Acid on Force Production in Rat Skeletal Muscle," *The Journal of Physiology*, 2001

In other words: Many scientists think that lactic acid causes muscle fatigue, but our evidence shows that it actually promotes recovery. Notice that the authors frame their claim with a version of the "they say / I say" formula: Although

previous work suggests _____, our data argue _____.
This basic move and its many variations are widespread in
scientific writing. The essential argumentative moves taught
in this book transcend disciplines, and the sciences are no
exception. The examples in this chaper were written by professional scientists, but they show moves that are appropriate in any writing that addresses scientific issues.

Despite the importance of argument in scientific writing,
newcomers to the genre often see it solely as a means for communicating uncontroversial, objective facts. It's easy to see how
this view arises. The objective tone of scientific writing can
obscure its argumentative nature, and many textbooks reinforce
a nonargumentative vision of science when they focus on
accepted conclusions and ignore ongoing controversies. And
because science writers base their arguments on empirical data,
a good portion of many scientific texts *does* serve the purpose
of delivering uncontested facts.

However, scientific writing often does more than just report
facts. Data are crucial to scientific argumentation, but they are
by no means the end of the story. Given important new data,
scientists assess their quality, draw conclusions from them, and
ponder their implications. They synthesize the new data with
existing information, propose novel theories, and design the
next experiments. In short, scientific progress depends on the
insight and creativity that scientists bring to their data. The
thrill of doing science, and writing about it, comes from the
ongoing struggle to use data to better understand our world.

START WITH THE DATA

Data are the fundamental currency of scientific argument.
Scientists develop hypotheses from existing data and then test

those by comparing their predictions to new experimental data. Summarizing data is therefore a basic move in science writing. Because data can often be interpreted in different ways, describing the data opens the door to critical analysis, creating opportunities to critique previous interpretations and develop new ones.

Describing data requires more than simply reporting numbers and conclusions. Rather than jumping straight to the punch line—to what X concluded—it is important first to describe the hypotheses, methods, and results that led to the conclusion: "To test the hypothesis that _____, X measured _____ and found that _____. Therefore, X concluded _____." In the following sections, we explore the three key rhetorical moves for describing the data that underpin a scientific argument: presenting the prevailing theories, explaining methodologies, and summarizing findings.

See how a physicist begins with data on pp. 206–13.

Present the Prevailing Theories

Readers must understand the prevailing theories that a study responds to before they can fully appreciate the details. So before diving into specifics, place the work in context by describing the prevailing theories and hypotheses. In the following passage from a 2004 journal article about insect respiration, the authors discuss an explanation for discontinuous gas exchange (DGC), a phenomenon where insects periodically close valves on their breathing tubes.

Lighton (1996, 1998; see also Lighton and Berrigan, 1995) noted the prevalence of DGC in fossorial insects, which inhabit microclimates where CO_2 levels may be relatively high. Consequently, Lighton proposed the chthonic hypothesis, which suggests that

DGC originated as a mechanism to improve gas exchange while
at the same time minimizing respiratory water loss.

A. G. GIBBS AND R. A. JOHNSON, "The Role of Discontinuous
Gas Exchange in Insects: The Chthonic Hypothesis Does Not
Hold Water," *The Journal of Experimental Biology*, 2004

Notice that Gibbs and Johnson not only describe Lighton's
hypothesis but also recap the evidence that supports it. By presenting this evidence, Gibbs and Johnson set the stage for
engaging with Lighton's ideas. For example, they might question the chthonic hypothesis by pointing out shortcomings of
the data or flaws in its interpretation. Or they might suggest
new approaches that could verify the hypothesis. The point is
that by incorporating a discussion of experimental findings into
their summary of Lighton's hypothesis, Gibbs and Johnson open
the door to a conversation with Lighton.

Here are some templates for presenting the data that underpin prevailing explanations:

▸ Experiments showing ＿＿＿＿ and ＿＿＿＿ have led scientists to propose ＿＿＿＿.

▸ Although most scientists attribute ＿＿＿＿ to ＿＿＿＿, X's
result ＿＿＿＿ leads to the possibility that ＿＿＿＿.

Explain the Methods

Even as we've argued that scientific arguments hinge on data, it's
important to note that the quality of data varies depending on
how they were collected. Data obtained with sloppy techniques
or poorly designed experiments could lead to faulty conclusions.
Therefore, it's crucial to explain the methods used to collect data.
In order for readers to evaluate a method, you'll need to indicate

its purpose, as the following passage from a journal article about the evolution of bird digestive systems demonstrates:

> To test the hypothesis that flowerpiercers have converged with hummingbirds in digestive traits, we compared the activity of intestinal enzymes and the gut nominal area of cinnamon-bellied flowerpiercers (Diglossa baritula) with those of eleven hummingbird species.
>
> J. E. SCHONDUBE AND C. MARTINEZ DEL RIO,
> *Journal of Comparative Physiology*, 2004

You need to indicate purpose whether describing your own work or that of others. Here are a couple of templates for doing so:

▶ Smith and colleagues evaluated _____ to determine whether _____ .

▶ Because _____ does not account for _____ , we instead used _____ .

Summarize the Findings

Scientific data often come in the form of numbers. Your task when presenting numerical data is to provide the context readers need to understand the numbers—by giving supporting information and making comparisons. In the following passage from a book about the interaction between organisms and their environments, Turner uses numerical data to support an argument about the role of the sun's energy on Earth.

> The potential rate of energy transfer from the Sun to Earth is prodigious—about 600 W m^{-2}, averaged throughout the year. Of this, only a relatively small fraction, on the order of 1–2 percent, is captured by green plants. The rest, if it is not reflected back into space, is available to do other things. The excess can be considerable: although some natural surfaces reflect as much as 95% of the

incoming solar beam, many natural surfaces reflect much less (Table 3.2), on average about 15–20 percent. The remaining absorbed energy is then capable of doing work, like heating up surfaces, moving water and air masses around to drive weather and climate, evaporating water, and so forth.

J. S. TURNER, The Extended Organism, 2000

Turner supports his point that a huge amount of the sun's energy is directly converted to work on Earth by quoting an actual value (600) with units of measurement (W m^{-2}, watts per square meter). Readers need the units to evaluate the value; 600 watts per square inch is very different from 600 W m^{-2}. Turner then makes comparisons using percent values, saying that only 1 to 2 percent of the total energy that reaches Earth is trapped by plants. Finally, Turner describes the data's variability by reporting comparisons as ranges—1 to 2 percent and 15 to 20 percent—rather than single values.

Supporting information—such as units of measurement, sample size (n), and amount of variability—helps readers assess the data. In general, the reliability of data improves as its sample size increases and its variability decreases. Supporting information can be concisely presented as:

▸ _____ ± _____ (*mean ± variability*) _____ (*units*), n = _____ (*sample size*).

For example: Before training, resting heart rate of the subjects was 56 ± 7 beats per minute, n = 12. Here's another way to give supporting information:

▸ We measured _____ (*sample size*) subjects, and the average response was _____ (*mean with units*) with a range of _____ (*lower value*) to _____ (*upper value*).

To help readers understand the data, make comparisons with values from the same study or from other similar work.

Here are some templates for making comparisons:

▸ Before training, average running speed was _____ ± _____ kilometers per hour, _____ kilometers per hour slower than running speed after training.

▸ We found athletes' heart rates to be _____ ± _____% lower than nonathletes'.

▸ The subjects in X's study completed the maze in _____ ± _____ seconds, _____ seconds slower than those in Y's study.

You will sometimes need to present qualitative data, such as that found in some images and photographs, that cannot be reduced to numbers. Qualitative data must be described precisely with words. In the passage below from a review article about connections between cellular protein localization and cell growth, the author describes the exact locations of three proteins: Scrib, Dlg, and Lgl.

Epithelial cells accumulate different proteins on their apical (top) and basolateral (bottom) surfaces. . . . Scrib and Dlg are localized at the septate junctions along the lateral cell surface, whereas Lgl coats vesicles that are found both in the cytoplasm and "docked" at the lateral surface of the cell.

M. PEIFER, "Travel Bulletin—Traffic Jams
Cause Tumors," *Science*, 2000

Explain What the Data Mean

Once you summarize experiments and results, you need to say what the data mean. Consider the following passage from a study in which scientists fertilized plots of tropical rainforest with nitrogen (N) and/or phosphorus (P).

> Although our data suggest that the mechanisms driving the observed respiratory responses to increased N and P may be different, the large CO_2 losses stimulated by N and P fertilization suggest that knowledge of such patterns and their effects on soil CO_2 efflux is critical for understanding the role of tropical forests in a rapidly changing global C [carbon] cycle.
>
> C. C. Cleveland and A. R. Townsend, "Nutrient Additions to a Tropical Rain Forest Drive Substantial Soil Carbon Dioxide Losses to the Atmosphere," *Proceedings of the National Academy of Sciences*, 2006

Notice that in discussing the implications of their data, Cleveland and Townsend use language—including the verbs "suggest" and "may be"—that denotes their level of confidence.

Whether you are summarizing what others say about their data or offering your own interpretation, pay attention to the verbs that connect data to interpretations.

To signify a moderate level of confidence:

▸ The data *suggest/hint/imply* _____.

To express a greater degree of certainty:

▸ Our results *show/demonstrate* _____.

Almost never will you use the verb "prove" in reference to a single study, because even very powerful evidence generally falls short of proof unless other studies support the same conclusion.

Scientific consensus arises when multiple studies point toward the same conclusion; conversely, contradictions among studies often signal research questions that need further work. For these reasons, you may need to compare one study's findings to those of another study. Here, too, you'll need to choose your verbs carefully.

▸ Our data *support/confirm/verify* the work of X by showing that _____.

▸ By demonstrating _____, X's work *extends* the findings of Y.

▸ The results of X *contradict/refute* Y's conclusion that _____.

▸ X's findings *call into question* the widely accepted theory that _____.

▸ Our data *are consistent with* X's hypothesis that _____.

MAKE YOUR OWN ARGUMENTS

Now we turn toward the part of scientific writing where you express your own opinions. One challenge is that the statements of other scientists about their methods and results usually must be accepted. You probably can't argue, for example, that "X and Y claim to have studied 6 elephants, but I think they actually only studied 4." However, it might be fair to say, "X and Y studied only 6 elephants, and this small sample size casts doubts on their conclusions." The second statement doesn't question what the scientists did or found but instead examines how the findings are interpreted.

When developing your own arguments—the "I say"—you will often start by assessing the interpretations of other scientists. Consider the following example from a review article about the beneficial acclimation hypothesis (BAH), the idea that organisms exposed to a particular environment become better suited to that environment than unexposed animals.

> To the surprise of most physiologists, all empirical examinations of the BAH have rejected its generality. However, we suggest that these examinations are neither direct nor complete tests of the functional benefit of acclimation.
>
> R. S. WILSON AND C. E. FRANKLIN, "Testing the Beneficial Acclimation Hypothesis," *Trends in Ecology & Evolution*, 2002

For more on the "twist it" move, see p. 60. Wilson and Franklin use a version of the "twist it" move: They acknowledge the data collected by other physiologists but question how those data have been interpreted, creating an opportunity to offer their own interpretation.

You might ask whether we should question how other scientists interpret their own work. Having conducted a study, aren't they in the best position to evaluate it? Perhaps, but as the above example demonstrates, other scientists might see the work from a different perspective or through more objective eyes. And in fact the culture of science depends on vigorous debate in which scientists defend their own findings and challenge those of others—a give and take that helps improve science's reliability. So expressing a critical view about someone else's work is an integral part of the scientific process. Let's examine some of the basic moves for entering scientific conversations: agreeing, with a difference; disagreeing and explaining why; simultaneously agreeing and disagreeing; anticipating objections; and saying why it matters.

Agree, but with a Difference

Scientific research passes through several levels of critical analysis before being published. Scientists get feedback when they discuss work with colleagues, present findings at conferences, and receive reviews of their manuscripts. So the juiciest debates may have been resolved before publication, and you may find little to disagree with in the published literature of a research field. Yet even if you agree with what you've read, there are still ways to join the conversation—and reasons to do so.

One approach is to suggest that further work should be done:

▸ Now that ＿＿＿＿＿ has been established, scientists will likely turn their attention toward ＿＿＿＿＿.

▸ X's work leads to the question of ＿＿＿＿＿. Therefore, we investigated ＿＿＿＿＿.

▸ To see whether these findings apply to ＿＿＿＿＿, we propose to ＿＿＿＿＿.

Another way to agree and at the same time jump into the conversation is to concur with a finding and then propose a mechanism that explains it. In the following sentence from a review article about dietary deficiencies, the author agrees with a previous finding and offers a probable explanation.

> Inadequate dietary intakes of vitamins and minerals are widespread, most likely due to excessive consumption of energy-rich, micronutrient-poor, refined food.
>
> B. AMES, "Low Micronutrient Intake May Accelerate the Degenerative Diseases of Aging through Allocation of Scarce Micronutrients by Triage," *Proceedings of the National Academy of Sciences*, 2006

Here are some templates for explaining an experimental result.

▸ One explanation for X's finding of _____ is that _____.
An alternative explanation is _____.

▸ The difference between _____ and _____ is probably due
to _____.

Disagree—and Explain Why

Although scientific consensus is common, healthy disagreement is not unusual. While measurements conducted by different teams of scientists under the same conditions should
produce the same result, scientists often disagree about which
techniques are most appropriate, how well an experimental
design tests a hypothesis, and how results should be interpreted. To illustrate such disagreement, let's return to the
debate about whether or not lactic acid is beneficial during
exercise. In the following passage, Lamb and Stephenson are
responding to work by Kristensen and colleagues, which
argues that lactic acid might be beneficial to resting muscle
but not to active muscle.

The argument put forward by Kristensen and colleagues (12) . . .
is not valid because it is based on observations made with isolated
whole soleus muscles that were stimulated at such a high rate that
>60% of the preparation would have rapidly become completely
anoxic (4). . . . Furthermore, there is no reason to expect that
adding more H+ to that already being generated by the muscle
activity should in any way be advantageous. It is a bit like opening up the carburetor on a car to let in too much air or throwing

gasoline over the engine and then concluding that air and gasoline are deleterious to engine performance.

G. D. Lamb and D. G. Stephenson,
"Point: Lactic Acid Accumulation Is an Advantage during
Muscle Activity," *Journal of Applied Physiology*, 2006

Lamb and Stephenson bring experimental detail to bear on their disagreement with Kristensen and colleagues. First, they criticize methodology, arguing that the high muscle stimulation rate used by Kristensen and colleagues created very low oxygen levels (anoxia). They also criticize the logic of the experimental design, arguing that adding more acid (H^+) to a muscle that is already producing it isn't informative. It's also worth noting how they drive home their point, likening Kristensen and colleagues' methodology to flooding an engine with air or gasoline. Even in technical scientific writing, you don't need to set aside your own voice completely.

In considering the work of others, look for instances where the experimental design and methodology fail to adequately test a hypothesis.

▸ The work of Y and Z appears to show that _____, but their experimental design does not control for _____ .

Also, consider the possibility that results do not lead to the stated conclusions.

► While X and Y claim that _____, their finding of _____ actually shows that _____ .

Okay, but . . .

Science tends to progress incrementally. New work may refine or extend previous work but doesn't often completely overturn it. For this reason, science writers frequently agree up to a point and then express some disagreement. In the following example from a commentary about methods for assessing how proteins interact, the authors acknowledge the value of the two-hybrid studies, but they also point out their shortcomings.

> The two-hybrid studies that produced the protein interaction map for *D. melanogaster* (12) provide a valuable genome-wide view of protein interactions but have a number of shortcomings (13). Even if the protein-protein interactions were determined with high accuracy, the resulting network would still require careful interpretation to extract its underlying biological meaning. Specifically, the map is a representation of all possible interactions, but one would only expect some fraction to be operating at any given time.
>
> J. J. RICE, A. KERSHENBAUM, AND G. STOLOVITZKY, "Lasting Impressions: Motifs in Protein-Protein Maps May Provide Footprints of Evolutionary Events." *Proceedings of the National Academy of Sciences*, 2005

Delineating the boundaries or limitations of a study is a good way to agree up to a point. Here are some templates for doing so.

▸ While X's work clearly demonstrates _____, _____ will be required before we can determine whether _____ .

▸ Although Y and Z present firm evidence for _____, their data can not be used to argue that _____ .

▸ In summary, our studies show that _____, but the issue of _____ remains unresolved.

Anticipate Objections

Skepticism is a key ingredient in the scientific process. Before an explanation is accepted, scientists demand convincing evidence and assess whether alternative explanations have been thoroughly explored, so it's essential that scientists consider possible objections to their ideas before presenting them. In the following example from a book about the origin of the universe, Tyson and Goldsmith first admit that some might doubt the existence of the poorly understood "dark matter" that physicists have proposed, and then they go on to respond to the skeptics.

> Unrelenting skeptics might compare the dark matter of today with the hypothetical, now defunct "ether," proposed centuries ago as the weightless, transparent medium through which light moved. . . . But dark matter ignorance differs fundamentally from ether ignorance. While ether amounted to a placeholder for our incomplete understanding, the existence of dark matter derives from not from mere presumption but from the observed effects of its gravity on visible matter.
>
> N. D. TYSON AND D. GOLDSMITH, *Origins: Fourteen Billion Years of Cosmic Evolution*, 2004

Anticipating objections in your own writing will help you clarify and address potential criticisms. Consider objections to your overall approach, as well as to specific aspects of your interpretations. Here are some templates for doing so.

▶ Scientists who take a _____ (*reductionist/integrative/ biochemical/computational/statistical*) approach might view our results differently.

▸ This interpretation of the data might be criticized by X, who has argued that _____.

▸ Some may argue that this experimental design fails to account for _____.

Say Why It Matters

Though individual studies can be narrowly focused, science ultimately seeks to answer big questions and produce useful technologies. So it's essential when you enter a scientific conversation to say why the work—and your arguments about it—matter. The following passage from a commentary on a research article notes two implications of work that evaluated the shape of electron orbitals.

> The classic textbook shape of electron orbitals has now been directly observed. As well as confirming the established theory, this work may be a first step to understanding high-temperature superconductivity.
>
> C. J. HUMPHREYS, "Electrons Seen in Orbit," *Nature*, 1999

Humphreys argues that the study confirms an established theory and that it may lead to better understanding in another area. When thinking about the broad significance of a study, consider both the practical applications and the impact on future scientific work.

▸ These results open the door to studies that _____.

▸ The methodologies developed by X will be useful for _____.

▸ Our findings are the first step toward _____ .

▸ Further work in this area may lead to the development of _____ .

READING AS A WAY OF ENTERING THE SCIENTIFIC CONVERSATION

In science, as in other disciplines, you'll often start with work done by others, and therefore you will need to critically evaluate their work. To that end, you'll need to probe how well their data support their interpretations. Doing so will lead you toward your own interpretations—your ticket into an ongoing scientific conversation. Here are some questions that will help you read and respond to scientific research.

How well do the methods test the hypothesis?

▸ Is the sample size adequate?

▸ Is the experimental design valid?
Were the proper controls performed?

▸ What are the limitations of the methodology?

▸ Are other techniques available?

How fairly have the results been interpreted?

▸ How well do the results support the stated conclusion?

▸ Has the data's variability been adequately considered?

▸ Do other findings verify (or contradict) the conclusion?

▸ What other experiments could test the conclusion?

What are the broader implications of the work?
Why does it matter?

- Can the results be generalized beyond the system that was studied?
- What are the work's practical implications?
- What questions arise from the work?
- Which experiments should be done next?

The examples in this chapter show that scientists do more than simply collect facts; they also interpret those facts and make arguments about their meaning. On the frontiers of science, where we are probing questions that are just beyond our capacity to answer, the data are inevitably incomplete and controversy is to be expected. Writing about science presents the opportunity to add your own arguments to the ongoing discussion.

FOURTEEN

"ANALYZE THIS"

Writing in the Social Sciences

ERIN ACKERMAN

—◻—

SOCIAL SCIENCE is the study of people—how they behave and relate to one another, and the organizations and institutions that facilitate these interactions. People are complicated, so any study of human behavior is at best partial, taking into account some elements of what people do and why, but not always explaining those actions definitively. As a result, it is the subject of constant conversation and argument.

Consider some of the topics studied in the social sciences: minimum wage laws, violence against women, tobacco regulation, the 2000 election, employment discrimination. Got an opinion on any of these topics? You aren't alone. But in the writing you do as a student of the social sciences, you need to

ERIN ACKERMAN is a professor of political science at John Jay College, City University of New York. Her research and teaching interests include American and comparative constitutional law, women and law, the law and politics of reproductive health, biomedical policy, and American political development.

write about more than just your opinions. Good writing in the social sciences, as in other academic disciplines, requires that you demonstrate that you have thought about what it is you think. The best way to do that is to bring your views into conversation with those expressed by others and to test what you and others think against a review of data. In other words, you'll need to start with what others say and then present what you say as a response.

Consider the following example from a book about contemporary American political culture:

> Claims of deep national division were standard fare after the 2000 elections, and to our knowledge few commentators have publicly challenged them. . . . In sum, contemporary observers of American politics have apparently reached a new consensus around the proposition that old disagreements about economics now pale in comparison to new divisions based on sexuality, morality, and religion, divisions so deep as to justify fears of violence and talk of war in describing them.
>
> This short book advocates a contrary thesis: the sentiments expressed in the previously quoted pronouncements of scholars, journalists, and politicos range from simple exaggeration to sheer nonsense. . . . Many of the activists in the political parties and various cause groups do, in fact, hate each other and regard themselves as combatants in a war. But their hatreds and battles are not shared by the great mass of the American people. . . .
>
> MORRIS P. FIORINA, *Culture War?*
> *The Myth of a Polarized America*, 2004

In other words, "they" (journalists, pundits, other political scientists) say that the American public is deeply divided, whereas Fiorina replies that they have misinterpreted the evidence—

specifically, that they have generalized from a few exceptional cases (activists). Even the title of the book calls into question an idea held by others, one Fiorina labels a "myth."

This chapter explores some of the basic moves social science writers make. In addition, writing in the social sciences generally includes several core components: a strong introduction and thesis, a literature review, and the writer's own analysis, including presentation of data and consideration of implications. Much of your own writing will include one or more of these components as well. The introduction sets out the thesis, or point, of the paper, briefly explaining what you will say in your text and how it fits into the preexisting conversation. The literature review summarizes what has already been said on your topic. Your analysis allows you to present data—the information about human behavior you are measuring or testing against what other people have said—and to explain the conclusions you have drawn based on your investigation. Do you agree, disagree, or some combination of both, with what has been said by others? What reasons can you give for why you feel that way? And so what? Who should be interested in what you have to say, and why?

THE INTRODUCTION AND THESIS: "THIS PAPER CHALLENGES . . ."

Your introduction sets forth what you plan to say in your essay. You might evaluate the work of earlier scholars or certain widely held assumptions and find them incorrect when measured against new data. Alternatively, you might point out that an author's work is largely correct, but that it could use some qualifications or be extended in some way. Or you might identify a gap in our knowledge—we know a great deal about topic

X but almost nothing about some other closely related topic. In each of these instances, your introduction needs to cover both "they say" and "I say" perspectives. If you stop after the "they say," your readers won't know what you are bringing to the conversation. Similarly, if you were to jump right to the "I say" portion of your argument, readers might wonder why you need to say anything at all.

Sometimes you join the conversation at a point where the discussion seems settled. One or more views about a topic have become so widely accepted among a group of scholars or society at large that these views are essentially the conventional way of thinking about the topic. You may wish to offer new reasons to support this interpretation, or you may wish to call these standard views into question. To do so, you must first introduce and identify these widely held beliefs and then present your own view. In fact, much of the writing in the social sciences takes the form of calling into question that which we think we already know. Consider the following example from a 2001 article from *The Journal of Economics Perspectives:*

> Fifteen years ago, Milton Friedman's 1957 treatise A *Theory of the Consumption Function* seemed badly dated. Dynamic optimization theory had not been employed much in economics when Friedman wrote, and utility theory was still comparatively primitive, so his statement of the "permanent income hypothesis" never actually specified a formal mathematical model of behavior derived explicitly from utility maximization . . . [W]hen other economists subsequently found multiperiod maximizing models that could be solved explicitly, the implications of those models differed sharply from Friedman's intuitive description of his "model." Furthermore, empirical tests in the 1970s and 1980s often rejected these rigorous versions of the permanent income hypothesis in favor of an

alternative hypothesis that many households simply spent all of their current income.

Today, with the benefit of a further round of mathematical (and computational) advances, Friedman's (1957) original analysis looks more prescient than primitive . . .

CHRISTOPHER D. CARROLL, "A Theory of Consumption
Function, With and Without Liquidity Constraints,"
The Journal of Economic Perspectives, 2001

This introduction makes clear that Carroll will defend Milton Friedman against some major criticisms of his work. Carroll mentions what has been said about Friedman's work and then goes on to say that the critiques turn out to be wrong and to suggest that Friedman's work reemerges as persuasive. A template of Carroll's introduction might look something like this: Economics research in the last fifteen years suggested Friedman's 1957 treatise was _____ because _____ . In other words, they say that Friedman's work is not accurate because of _____ , _____ , and _____ . Recent research convinces me, however, that Friedman's work makes sense.

In some cases, however, there may not be a strong consensus among experts on a topic. You might enter the ongoing debate by casting your vote with one side or another or by offering an alternative view. In the following example, Shari Berman identifies two competing accounts of how to explain world events in the twentieth century and then puts forth a third view.

Conventional wisdom about twentieth-century ideologies rests on two simple narratives. One focuses on the struggle for dominance between democracy and its alternatives. . . . The other narrative focuses on the competition between free-market capitalism and its rivals. . . . Both of these narratives obviously contain some truth. . . . Yet both only tell part of the story, which is why their common conclusion—neoliberalism as the "end of History"—is unsatisfying and misleading.

What the two conventional narratives fail to mention is that a third struggle was also going on: between those ideologies that believed in the primacy of economics and those that believed in the primacy of politics.

SHARI BERMAN, "The Primacy of Economics versus the Primacy of Politics: Understanding the Ideological Dynamics of the Twentieth Century," *Perspectives on Politics*, 2009

After identifying the two competing narratives, Berman suggests a third view—and later goes on to argue that this third view explains current debates over globalization. A template for this type of introduction might look something like this: In recent discussions of _____, a controversial aspect has been _____. On the one hand, some argue that _____. On the other hand, others argue that _____. Neither of these arguments, however, considers the alternative view that _____.

Given the complexity of many of the issues studied in the social sciences, however, you may sometimes agree *and* disagree with existing views—pointing out things that you believe are correct or have merit, while disagreeing with or refining other points. In the example below, anthropologist Sally Engle Merry agrees with another scholar about something that is a key trait of modern society but argues that this trait has a different origin than the other author identifies.

For more on different ways of responding, see Chapter 4.

Although I agree with Rose that an increasing emphasis on governing the soul is characteristic of modern society, I see the transformation not as evolutionary but as the product of social mobilization and political struggle.

> SALLY ENGLE MERRY, "Rights, Religion, and Community:
> Approaches to Violence against Women in the
> Context of Globalization," *Law and Society Review*, 2001

Here are some templates for agreeing and disagreeing:

▶ Although I agree with X up to a point, I cannot accept his overall conclusion that ＿＿＿＿＿.

▶ Although I disagree with X on ＿＿＿＿＿ and ＿＿＿＿＿, I agree with her conclusion that ＿＿＿＿＿.

▶ Political scientists studying ＿＿＿＿＿ have argued that it is caused by ＿＿＿＿＿. While ＿＿＿＿＿ contributes to the problem, ＿＿＿＿＿ is also an important factor.

In the process of examining people from different angles, social scientists sometimes identify gaps—areas that have not been explored in previous research. In a 1998 article on African American neighborhoods, sociologist Mary Pattillo identifies such a gap.

The research on African Americans is dominated by inquiries into the lives of the black poor. Contemporary ethnographies and journalistic descriptions have thoroughly described deviance, gangs, drugs, intergender relations and sexuality, stymied aspiration, and family patterns in poor neighborhoods (Dash 1989; Hagedorn 1988; Kotlowitz 1991; Lemann 1991; MacLeod 1995; Sullivan 1989; Williams 1989). Yet, the majority of African Americans are not poor (Billingsley 1992). A significant part of the black experience, namely that of working and middle-class blacks, remains unexplored. We have little information about what black middle-class neighborhoods look like and how social life is organized within them. . . . this article begins to fill this empirical and theoretical gap using ethnographic data collected in Groveland, a middle-class black neighborhood in Chicago.

MARY E. PATTILLO, "Sweet Mothers and Gangbangers: Managing Crime in a Black Middle-Class Neighborhood," *Social Forces*, 1998

Pattillo explains that much has been said about poor African American neighborhoods. But, she says, we have little information about the experience of working-class and middle-class black neighborhoods—a gap that her article will address.

Here are some templates for introducing gaps in the existing research:

▸ Studies of X have indicated _____. It is not clear, however, that this conclusion applies to _____.

▸ _____ often take for granted that _____. Few have investigated this assumption, however.

▸ X's work tells us a great deal about _____. Can this work be generalized to _____?

Again, a good introduction indicates what you have to say in the larger context of what others have said. Throughout the rest of your paper, you will move back and forth between the "they say" and the "I say," adding more details.

The Literature Review:
"Prior Research Indicates . . ."

In the literature review, you explain what "they say" in more detail, summarizing, paraphrasing, or quoting the viewpoints to which you are responding. But you need to balance what they are saying with your own focus. You need to characterize someone else's work fairly and accurately but set up the points you yourself want to make by selecting the details that are relevant to your own perspective and observations.

It is common in the social sciences to summarize several arguments at once, identifying their major arguments or findings in a single paragraph.

How do employers in a low-wage labor market respond to an increase in the minimum wage? The prediction from conventional economic theory is unambiguous: a rise in the minimum wage leads perfectly competitive employers to cut employment (George J. Stigler, 1946). Although studies in the 1970's based on aggregate teenage employment rates usually confirmed this prediction, earlier studies based on comparisons of employment at affected and unaffected establishments often did not (e.g., Richard A. Lester, 1960, 1964). Several recent studies that rely on a similar comparative methodology have failed to detect a negative employment effect of higher minimum wages. Analyses of the 1990–1991 increases in the federal minimum wage (Lawrence F. Katz and Krueger, 1992; Card, 1992a) and of an earlier increase in the minimum wage in California (Card, 1992b) find no adverse employment impact.

David Card and Alan Krueger,
"Minimum Wages and Employment: A Case Study of the
Fast-Food Industry in New Jersey and Pennsylvania,"
The American Economic Review, 1994;

Card and Krueger cite the key findings and conclusions of works that are relevant to the question they are investigating and the point they plan to address, asking "How do employers in a low-wage labor market respond to an increase in the minimum wage?" They go on, as good writers should, to answer the question they ask. And they do so by reviewing others who have answered that question, noting that this question has been answered in different, sometimes contradictory, ways.

Such summaries are brief, bringing together relevant arguments by several scholars to provide an overview of scholarly work on a particular topic. In writing such a summary, you need to ask yourself how the authors themselves might describe their positions and also consider what in their work is relevant for the point you wish to make. This kind of summary is especially appropriate when you have a large amount of research material on a topic and want to identify the major strands of a debate or to show how the work of one author builds on that of another. Here are some templates for overview summaries:

▸ In addressing the question of _____, political scientists have considered several explanations for _____. X argues that _____. According to Y and Z, another plausible explanation is _____.

▸ What is the effect of _____ on _____? Previous work on _____ by X and by Y and Z supports _____.

Sometimes you may need to say more about the works you cite. On a midterm or final exam, for example, you may need to demonstrate that you have a deep familiarity with a particular work. And in some disciplines of the social sciences, longer, more detailed literature reviews are the standard. Your instructor and the articles he or she has assigned are your best guides for the length and level of detail of your literature review. Other times, the work of certain authors is especially important for your argument, and therefore you need to provide more details to explain what these authors have said. See how Martha Derthick summarizes an argument that is central to her 2001 book about the politics of tobacco regulation.

> The idea that governments could sue to reclaim health care costs from cigarette manufacturers might be traced to "Cigarettes and Welfare Reform," an article published in the *Emory Law Journal* in 1977 by Donald Gasner, a law professor at the University of Southern Illinois. Garner suggested that state governments could get a cigarette manufacturer to pay the direct medical costs "of looking after patients with smoking diseases." He drew an analogy to the Coal Mine Health and Safety Act of 1969, under which coal mine operators are required to pay certain disability benefits for coal miners suffering from pneumoconiosis, or black lung disease.
>
> MARTHA DERTHICK, *Up In Smoke: From Legislation to Litigation in Tobacco Politics*, 2005

Note that Derthick identifies the argument she is summarizing, quoting its author directly and then adding details about a precedent for the argument.

You may want to include direct quotations of what others have said, as Derthick does. Using an author's exact words helps you demonstrate that you are representing him or her fairly. But you cannot simply insert a quotation, you need to explain to your readers what it means for your point. Consider the following example drawn from a 2004 political science book on the debate over tort reform.

> The essence of *agenda setting* was well enunciated by E. E. Schattschneider: "In politics as in everything else, it makes a great

difference whose game we play" (1960, 47). In short, the ability to define or control the rules, terms, or perceived options in a contest over policy greatly affects the prospects for winning."

WILLIAM HALTOM AND MICHAEL McCANN, *Distorting the Law: Politics, Media, and the Litigation Crisis*, 2004

Notice how Haltom and McCann first quote Schattschneider and then explain in their own words how political agenda setting can be thought of as a game, with winners and losers.

Remember that whenever you summarize, quote, or paraphrase the work of others, credit must be given in the form of a citation to the original work. The words may be your own, but if the idea comes from someone else you must give credit to the original work. There are several formats for documenting sources. Consult your instructor for help choosing which citation style to use.

THE ANALYSIS

The literature review covers what others have said on your topic. The analysis allows you to present and support your own response. In the introduction you indicate whether you agree, disagree, or some combination of both with what others have said. You will want to expand on how you have formed your opinion and why others should care about your topic.

"The Data Indicate . . ."

The social sciences use data to develop and test explanations. Data can be quantitative or qualitative and can come from a number of sources. You might use statistics related to GDP growth, unemployment, voting rates, or demographics. Or you could use surveys, interviews, or other first-person accounts.

Regardless of the type of data used, it is important to do three things: define your data, indicate where you got the data, and then say what you have done with your data. In a 2005 journal article, political scientist Joshua C. Wilson examines a court case about protests at an abortion clinic and asks whether each side of the conflict acts in a way consistent with their general views on freedom of speech.

[T]his paper relies on close readings of in-person, semi-structured interviews with the participants involved in the real controversy that was the *Williams* case.

Thirteen interviews ranging in length from 40 minutes to 1 hour and 50 minutes were conducted for this paper. Of those interviewed, all would be considered "elites" in terms of political psychology/political attitude research—six were active members of Solano Citizens for Life . . . ; two were members of Planned Parenthood Shasta-Diablo management; one was the lawyer who obtained the restraining order, temporary injunction, and permanent injunction for Planned parenthood; one was the lawyer for the duration of the case for Solano Citizens for life; two were lawyers for Planned Parenthood on appeal; and one was the Superior Court judge who heard arguments for, and finally crafted, the restraining order and injunctions against Solano Citizens for Life. During the course of the interviews, participants were asked a range of questions about their experiences and thoughts in relation to the *Williams* case, as well as their beliefs about the interpretation and limits of the First Amendment right to free speech—both in general, and in relation to the Williams case.

JOSHUA C. WILSON. "When Rights Collide: Anti-Abortion Protests and the Ideological Dilemma in *Planned Parenthood Shasta-Diablo, Inc. v. Williams*," *Studies in Law, Politics, and Society*, 2005

Wilson identifies and describes his qualitative data—interviews conducted with key parties in the conflict—and explains the nature of the questions he asked.

If your data are quantitative, you will need to explain them similarly. See how political scientist Brian Arbour explains the quantitative data he used to study for a 2009 article in *The Forum* how a change of rules might have affected the outcome of the 2008 Democratic primary contest between Hillary Clinton and Barack Obama.

> I evaluate these five concerns about the Democratic system of delegate allocation by "rerunning" the Obama-Clinton contest with a different set of allocation rules, those in effect for the 2008 Republican presidential contest. . . . Republicans allow each state to make their own rules, leading to "a plethora of selection plans" (Shapiro & Bello 2008, 5) . . . To "rerun" the Democratic primary under Republican rules, I need data on the results of the Democratic primary for each state and congressional district and on the Republican delegate allocation rules for each state. The Green Papers (www.thegreenpapers.com), a website that serves as an almanac of election procedures, rules, and results, provides each of these data sources. By "rerunning" the Democratic primaries and caucuses, I use the exact results of each contest.
>
> BRIAN ARBOUR, "Even Closer, Even Longer: What If the 2008 Democratic Primary Used Republican Rules?" *The Forum*, 2009

Note that Arbour identifies his data as primary voting results and the rules for Republican primaries. In the rest of the paper, Arbour shows how his use of these data suggests that political commentators who thought Republican rules would have clarified the close race between Clinton and Obama were wrong and the race would have been "even closer, even longer."

Here are some templates for discussing data:

▸ In order to test the hypothesis that _____, we assessed _____. Our calculations suggest _____.

▸ I used _____ to investigate _____. The results of this investigation indicate _____.

"But Others May Object . . ."

No matter how strongly your data support your argument, there are almost surely other perspectives (and thus other data) that you need to acknowledge. By considering possible objections to your argument and taking them seriously, you demonstrate that you've done your work and that you're aware of other perspectives—and most important, you present your own argument as part of an ongoing conversation.

See how economist Christopher Carroll acknowledges that there may be objections to his argument about how people allocate their income between consumption and savings.

I have argued here that the modern version of the dynamically optimizing consumption model is able to match many of the important features of the empirical data on consumption and saving behavior. There are, however, several remaining reasons for discomfort with the model.

CHRISTOPHER D. CARROLL, "A Theory of Consumption Function, With and Without Liquidity Constraints," *The Journal of Economic Perspectives*, 2001

Carroll then goes on to identify the possible limitations of his mathematical analysis.

Someone may object because there are related phenomena that your analysis does not explain or because you do not have the right data to investigate a particular question. Or perhaps someone may object to assumptions underlying your argument or how you handled your data. Here are some templates for considering naysayers:

▶ _____ might object that _____.

▶ Is my claim realistic? I have argued _____, but readers may question _____.

▶ My explanation accounts for _____ but does not explain _____. This is because _____.

"Why Should We Care?"

Who should care about your research, and why? Since the social sciences attempt to explain human behavior, it is important to consider how your research affects the assumptions we make about human behavior. In addition, you might offer recommendations for how other social scientists might continue to explore an issue, or what actions policymakers should take.

In the following example, sociologist Devah Pager identifies the implications of her study of the way having a criminal record affects a person applying for jobs.

[I]n terms of policy implications, this research has troubling conclusions. In our frenzy of locking people up, our "crime control" policies may in fact exacerbate the very conditions that lead to crime in the first place. Research consistently shows that finding quality steady employment is one of the strongest predictors of desistance from crime (Shover 1996; Sampson and Laub 1993; Uggen 2000). The fact that a criminal record severely limits employment opportunities—particularly among blacks—suggests that these individuals are left with few viable alternatives.

DEVAH PAGER, "The Mark of a Criminal Record," *The American Journal of Sociology,* 2003

Pager's conclusion that a criminal record negatively affects employment chances creates a vicious circle, she says: steady employment discourages recidivism, but a criminal record makes it harder to get a job.

In answering the "so what?" question, you need to explain why your readers should care. Although sometimes the implications of your work may be so broad that they would be of interest to almost anyone, it's never a bad idea to identify explicitly any groups of people who will find your work important.

Templates for establishing why your claims matter:

▸ X is important because _____.

▸ Ultimately, what is at stake here is _____.

▸ The finding that _____ should be of interest to _____ because _____.

As noted at the beginning of this chapter, the complexity of people allows us to look at their behavior from many different viewpoints. Much has been, and will be, said about how and why people do the things they do. As a result, we can look at writing in the social sciences as an ongoing conversation.

When you join this conversation, the "they say / I say" framework will help you figure out what has already been said (they say) and what you can add (I say). The components of social science writing presented in this chapter are tools to help you join that conversation.

READINGS

Don't Blame the Eater

DAVID ZINCZENKO

—◻—

IF EVER THERE were a newspaper headline custom-made for Jay Leno's monologue, this was it. Kids taking on McDonald's this week, suing the company for making them fat. Isn't that like middle-aged men suing Porsche for making them get speeding tickets? Whatever happened to personal responsibility?

I tend to sympathize with these portly fast-food patrons, though. Maybe that's because I used to be one of them.

I grew up as a typical mid-1980s latchkey kid. My parents were split up, my dad off trying to rebuild his life, my mom working long hours to make the monthly bills. Lunch and dinner, for me, was a daily choice between McDonald's, Taco Bell, Kentucky Fried Chicken or Pizza Hut. Then as now, these were the only available options for an American kid to get an affordable meal. By age 15, I had packed 212 pounds of torpid teenage tallow on my once lanky 5-foot-10 frame.

Then I got lucky. I went to college, joined the Navy Reserves and got involved with a health magazine. I learned how to manage my diet. But most of the teenagers who live, as I once did,

DAVID ZINCZENKO is the editor-in-chief of *Men's Health*, a monthly magazine that focuses on fitness. This piece was first published on the op-ed page of the *New York Times* on November 23, 2002.

on a fast-food diet won't turn their lives around: They've crossed under the golden arches to a likely fate of lifetime obesity. And the problem isn't just theirs—it's all of ours.

Before 1994, diabetes in children was generally caused by a genetic disorder—only about 5 percent of childhood cases were obesity-related, or Type 2, diabetes. Today, according to the National Institutes of Health, Type 2 diabetes accounts for at least 30 percent of all new childhood cases of diabetes in this country.

For tips on saying why it matters, see Chapter 7.

Not surprisingly, money spent to treat diabetes has skyrocketed, too. The Centers for Disease Control and Prevention estimate that diabetes accounted for $2.6 billion in health care costs in 1969. Today's number is an unbelievable $100 billion a year.

Shouldn't we know better than to eat two meals a day in fast-food restaurants? That's one argument. But where, exactly, are consumers—particularly teenagers—supposed to find alternatives? Drive down any thoroughfare in America, and I guarantee you'll see one of our country's more than 13,000 McDonald's restaurants. Now, drive back up the block and try to find someplace to buy a grapefruit.

Complicating the lack of alternatives is the lack of information about what, exactly, we're consuming. There are no calorie information charts on fast-food packaging, the way there are on grocery items. Advertisements don't carry warning labels the way tobacco ads do. Prepared foods aren't covered under Food and Drug Administration labeling laws. Some fast-food purveyors will provide calorie information on request, but even that can be hard to understand.

For example, one company's Web site lists its chicken salad as containing 150 calories; the almonds and noodles that come with it (an additional 190 calories) are listed separately. Add a serving of the 280-calorie dressing, and you've got a healthy lunch alternative that comes in at 620 calories. But that's not all. Read the small print on the back of the dressing packet and you'll realize it actually contains 2.5 servings. If you pour what you've been served, you're suddenly up around 1,040 calories, which is half of the government's recommended daily calorie intake. And that doesn't take into account that 450-calorie super-size Coke.

Make fun if you will of these kids launching lawsuits against the fast-food industry, but don't be surprised if you're the next plaintiff. As with the tobacco industry, it may be only a matter of time before state governments begin to see a direct line between the $1 billion that McDonald's and Burger King spend each year on advertising and their own swelling health care costs.

And I'd say the industry is vulnerable. Fast-food companies are marketing to children a product with proven health hazards and no warning labels. They would do well to protect themselves, and their customers, by providing the nutrition information people need to make informed choices about their products. Without such warnings, we'll see more sick, obese children and more angry, litigious parents. I say, let the deep-fried chips fall where they may.

Hidden Intellectualism

GERALD GRAFF

—◱—

EVERYONE KNOWS SOME young person who is impressively
"street smart" but does poorly in school. What a waste, we
think, that one who is so intelligent about so many things in
life seems unable to apply that intelligence to academic work.
What doesn't occur to us, though, is that schools and colleges
might be at fault for missing the opportunity to tap into such
street smarts and channel them into good academic work.

Nor do we consider one of the major reasons why schools
and colleges overlook the intellectual potential of street smarts:
the fact that we associate those street smarts with anti-
intellectual concerns. We associate the educated life, the life
of the mind, too narrowly and exclusively with subjects and
texts that we consider inherently weighty and academic. We

GERALD GRAFF, one of the co-authors of this book, is a professor of
English and education at the University of Illinois at Chicago. He is
a past President of the Modern Language Association, a professional
association of scholars and teachers of English and other languages.
This essay is adapted from his 2003 book *Clueless in Academe: How
Schooling Obscures the Life of the Mind.*

assume that it's possible to wax intellectual about Plato, Shakespeare, the French Revolution, and nuclear fission, but not about cars, dating, fashion, sports, TV, or video games.

The trouble with this assumption is that no necessary connection has ever been established between any text or subject and the educational depth and weight of the discussion it can generate. Real intellectuals turn any subject, however lightweight it may seem, into grist for their mill through the thoughtful questions they bring to it, whereas a dullard will find a way to drain the interest out of the richest subject. That's why a George Orwell writing on the cultural meanings of penny postcards is infinitely more substantial than the cogitations of many professors on Shakespeare or globalization (104–16).

See pp. 58–61 for tips on disagreeing, with reasons.

Students do need to read models of intellectually challenging writing—and Orwell is a great one—if they are to become intellectuals themselves. But they would be more prone to take on intellectual identities if we encouraged them to do so at first on subjects that interest them rather than ones that interest us.

I offer my own adolescent experience as a case in point. 5 Until I entered college, I hated books and cared only for sports. The only reading I cared to do or could do was sports magazines, on which I became hooked, becoming a regular reader of *Sport* magazine in the late forties, *Sports Illustrated* when it began publishing in 1954, and the annual magazine guides to professional baseball, football, and basketball. I also loved the sports novels for boys of John R. Tunis and Clair Bee and autobiographies of sports stars like Joe DiMaggio's *Lucky to Be a Yankee* and Bob Feller's *Strikeout Story*. In short, I was your typical teenage anti-intellectual—or so I believed for a long time. I have recently come to think, however, that my preference for sports over schoolwork was not anti-intellectualism so much as intellectualism by other means.

In the Chicago neighborhood I grew up in, which had become a melting pot after World War II, our block was solidly middle class, but just a block away—doubtless concentrated there by the real estate companies—were African Americans, Native Americans, and "hillbilly" whites who had recently fled postwar joblessness in the South and Appalachia. Negotiating this class boundary was a tricky matter. On the one hand, it was necessary to maintain the boundary between "clean-cut" boys like me and working-class "hoods," as we called them, which meant that it was good to be openly smart in a book-ish sort of way. On the other hand, I was desperate for the approval of the hoods, whom I encountered daily on the play-ing field and in the neighborhood, and for this purpose it was not at all good to be book-smart. The hoods would turn on you if they sensed you were putting on airs over them: "Who you lookin' at, smart ass?" as a leather-jacketed youth once said to me as he relieved me of my pocket change along with my self-respect.

I grew up torn, then, between the need to prove I was smart and the fear of a beating if I proved it too well; between the need not to jeopardize my respectable future and the need to impress the hoods. As I lived it, the conflict came down to a choice between being physically tough and being verbal. For a boy in my neighborhood and elementary school, only being "tough" earned you complete legitimacy. I still recall endless, complicated debates in this period with my closest pals over who was "the toughest guy in the school." If you were less than negligible as a fighter, as I was, you set-tled for the next best thing, which was to be inarticulate, carefully hiding telltale marks of literacy like correct grammar and pronunciation.

In one way, then, it would be hard to imagine an adolescence more thoroughly anti-intellectual than mine. Yet in retrospect, I see that it's more complicated, that I and the 1950s themselves were not simply hostile toward intellectualism, but divided and ambivalent. When Marilyn Monroe married the playwright Arthur Miller in 1956 after divorcing the retired baseball star Joe DiMaggio, the symbolic triumph of geek over jock suggested the way the wind was blowing. Even Elvis, according to his biographer Peter Guralnick, turns out to have supported Adlai over Ike in the presidential election of 1956. "I don't dig the intellectual bit," he told reporters. "But I'm telling you, man, he knows the most" (327).

Though I too thought I did not "dig the intellectual bit," I see now that I was unwittingly in training for it. The germs had actually been planted in the seemingly philistine debates about which boys were the toughest. I see now that in the interminable analysis of sports teams, movies, and toughness that my friends and I engaged in—a type of analysis, needless to say, that the real toughs would never have stooped to—I was already betraying an allegiance to the egghead world. I was practicing being an intellectual before I knew that was what I wanted to be.

It was in these discussions with friends about toughness and 10 sports, I think, and in my reading of sports books and magazines, that I began to learn the rudiments of the intellectual life: how to make an argument, weigh different kinds of evidence, move between particulars and generalizations, summarize the views of others, and enter a conversation about ideas. It was in reading and arguing about sports and toughness that

I experienced what it felt like to propose a generalization, restate and respond to a counterargument, and perform other intellectualizing operations, including composing the kind of sentences I am writing now.

Only much later did it dawn on me that the sports world was more compelling than school because it was *more intellectual than school,* not less. Sports after all was full of challenging arguments, debates, problems for analysis, and intricate statistics that you could care about, as school conspicuously was not. I believe that street smarts beat out book smarts in our culture not because street smarts are nonintellectual, as we generally suppose, but because they satisfy an intellectual thirst more thoroughly than school culture, which seems pale and unreal.

They also satisfy the thirst for community. When you entered sports debates, you became part of a community that was not limited to your family and friends, but was national and public. Whereas schoolwork isolated you from others, the pennant race or Ted Williams's .400 batting average was something you could talk about with people you had never met. Sports introduced you not only to a culture steeped in argument, but to a public argument culture that transcended the personal. I can't blame my schools for failing to make intellectual culture resemble the Super Bowl, but I do fault them for failing to learn anything from the sports and entertainment worlds about how to organize and represent intellectual culture, how to exploit its gamelike element and turn it into arresting public spectacle that might have competed more successfully for my youthful attention.

For here is another thing that never dawned on me and is still kept hidden from students, with tragic results: that the real intellectual world, the one that existed in the big world beyond school, is organized very much like the world of team sports, with rival texts, rival interpretations and evaluations of texts, rival theories of why they should be read and taught, and elaborate team competitions in which "fans" of writers, intellectual systems, methodologies, and -isms contend against each other.

To be sure, school contained plenty of competition, which became more invidious as one moved up the ladder (and has become even more so today with the advent of high-stakes testing). In this competition, points were scored not by making arguments, but by a show of information or vast reading, by grade-grubbing, or other forms of one-upmanship. School competition, in short, reproduced the less attractive features of sports culture without those that create close bonds and community.

And in distancing themselves from anything as enjoyable and absorbing as sports, my schools missed the opportunity to capitalize on an element of drama and conflict that the intellectual world shares with sports. Consequently, I failed to see the parallels between the sports and academic worlds that could have helped me cross more readily from one argument culture to the other.

Sports is only one of the domains whose potential for literacy training (and not only for males) is seriously underestimated by educators, who see sports as competing with academic development rather than a route to it. But if this argument suggests why it is a good idea to assign readings and topics that are close to students' existing interests, it also suggests the limits of this tactic. For students who get excited about the chance to write about their passion for cars will often write as poorly and unreflectively on that topic as on Shakespeare or Plato. Here is the flip side of what I pointed out before: that there's no necessary relation between the degree of interest a student shows in a text or subject and the quality of thought or expression such a student manifests in writing or talking about it. The challenge, as college professor Ned Laff has put it, "is not simply to exploit students' nonacademic interests, but to get them to see those interests through academic eyes."

To say that students need to see their interests "through academic eyes" is to say that street smarts are not enough. Making students' nonacademic interests an object of academic study is useful, then, for getting students' attention and overcoming their boredom and alienation, but this tactic won't in itself necessarily move them closer to an academically rigorous treatment of those interests. On the other hand, inviting students to write about cars, sports, or clothing fashions does not have to be a pedagogical cop-out as long as students are required to see these interests "through academic eyes," that is, to think and write about cars, sports, and fashions in a reflective, analytical way, one that sees them as microcosms of what is going on in the wider culture.

If I am right, then schools and colleges are missing an opportunity when they do not encourage students to take their nonacademic interests as objects of academic study. It is self-defeating to decline to introduce any text or subject that figures to engage students who will otherwise tune out academic work entirely. If a student cannot get interested in Mill's *On Liberty* but will read *Sports Illustrated* or *Vogue* or the hip-hop magazine *Source* with absorption, this is a strong argument for assigning the magazines over the classic. It's a good bet that if students get hooked on reading and writing by doing term papers on *Source*, they will eventually get to *On Liberty*. But even if they don't, the magazine reading will make them more literate and reflective than they would be otherwise. So it makes pedagogical sense to develop classroom units on sports, cars, fashions, rap music, and other such topics. Give me the student anytime who writes a sharply argued, sociologically acute analysis of an issue in *Source* over the student who writes a lifeless explication of *Hamlet* or Socrates' *Apology*.

Works Cited

Cramer, Richard Ben. *Joe DiMaggio: The Hero's Life.* New York: Simon and Schuster, 2000. Print.

DiMaggio, Joe. *Lucky to Be a Yankee.* New York: Bantam Books, 1949. Print.

Feller, Bob. *Strikeout Story*, New York: Bantam Books, 1948. Print.

Guralnick, Peter. *Last Train to Memphis: The Rise of Elvis Presley.* Boston: Little, Brown and Co., 1994. Print.

Orwell, George. *A Collection of Essays.* New York: Harcourt, Inc., 1953. Print.

Nuclear Waste

RICHARD A. MULLER

—▢—

As PEOPLE recognize the dangers of fossil fuel plants—especially the risk of global warming from carbon dioxide production—nuclear power begins to look more attractive. But what about the waste—all that highly radioactive debris that will endure for thousands of years? Do we have the right to leave such a legacy to our children?

Nuclear waste is one of the biggest technical issues that any future president is likely to face. The problem seems totally intractable. Plutonium—just one of the many highly radioactive waste products—has a half-life of 24,000 years. Even in that unimaginable amount of time, its intense radioactivity will decrease by only half. After 48,000 years it will still emit deadly radiation at a quarter of its original level. Even after 100,000 years the radiation will still be above 10% of the level it had when it left the reactor. What if it leaks into the ground and

RICHARD A. MULLER is professor of physics at the University of California at Berkeley. He is a past winner of the MacArthur Fellowship, often referred to as a "genius" award. This piece was given originally as a lecture in his physics course for non-science students and was then published in a collection of his course lectures, *Physics for Future Presidents* (2008).

reaches human water supplies? How can we possibly certify that this material can be kept safe for 100,000 years?

Still, the US government persists in its pursuit of "safe" nuclear waste disposal. It has created a prototype nuclear waste facility buried deep within Yucca Mountain, Nevada (Figure 1). To keep the waste safe, the storage rooms are 1000 feet below the surface. To store even part of the present nuclear waste requires a vast area, nearly 2 square miles. The cost of the facility is expected to reach $100 billion, with hundreds of billions of dollars more in operating costs.

To make matters worse, the Yucca Mountain region is seismically active. More than 600 earthquakes of magnitude 2.5 and higher have occurred within 50 miles in the last decade

Figure 1. Yucca Mountain, Nevada, the site of the prototype nuclear waste storage facility.

alone. Moreover, the region was created by volcanic activity. Although that was millions of years ago, how sure can we be that the waste facility won't be torn apart by another eruption?

Many alternatives have been suggested for nuclear waste storage. Why not just send the waste into the sun? Well, maybe that's not such a good idea, since on launch some rockets do crash back down on the Earth. Some scientists have proposed that the waste be put in vessels and sunk under the oceans, in a region where the movement of the Earth's crustal plates will subduct the material, eventually burying it hundreds of miles deep. Yet just the fact that scientists make such suggestions seems to emphasize how severe the problem really is.

Here is the worst part. We have already generated more than enough nuclear waste to fill up Yucca Mountain. That waste won't go away. Yet you, a future president, are considering *more* nuclear power? Are you insane?

My Confession

The furor against nuclear power has been so intense that I felt compelled to reproduce the anti-nuke viewpoint in the opening of this chapter, including at least part of their passion. These are the arguments that you will hear when you are president. Yet it hardly matters whether you are pro-nuke or anti-nuke. The waste is there, and you will have to do something with it. You can't ignore this issue, and to do the right thing (and to convince the public that you're doing the right thing) you must understand the physics.

When I work out the numbers, I find the dangers of storing our waste at Yucca Mountain to be small compared to the dangers of not doing so, and significantly smaller than many other dangers we ignore. Yet the contentious debate continues. More research is demanded, but every bit of additional research seems to raise new questions that exacerbate the public's fear and distrust. I have titled this section "My Confession" because I find it hard to stand aside and present the physics without giving my own personal evaluation. Through most of this book I've tried to present the facts, and just the facts, and let you draw the conclusions. In this section, I confess that I'll depart from that approach. I can't be evenhanded, because the facts seem to point strongly toward a particular conclusion.

I've discussed Yucca Mountain with scientists, politicians, and many concerned citizens. Most of the politicians believe the matter to be a scientific issue, and most of the scientists think it is political. Both are in favor of more research—scientists because that is what they do, and politicians because they think the research will answer the key questions. I don't think it will.

Here are some pertinent facts. The underground tunnels at Yucca Mountain are designed to hold 77,000 tons of high-level nuclear waste. Initially, the most dangerous part of this waste is not plutonium, but fission fragments such as strontium-90, an unstable nucleus created when the uranium nucleus splits. Because these fission fragments have shorter half-lives than uranium, the waste is about 1000 times more radioactive than the original **See Chapter 13 for tips on describing the data underpinning a scientific argument.** ore. It takes 10,000 years for the waste (not including plutonium, which is also produced in the reactor, and which I'll discuss later) to decay back to the radioactive level of the mined uranium. Largely on the basis of this number, people have searched for a site that will remain secure for 10,000 years. After that, we are better off than if we left the uranium in the ground, so 10,000 years of safety is probably good enough, not the 100,000 years that I mentioned in the chapter introduction.

Ten thousand years still seems impossibly long. What will the world be like 10,000 years from now? Think backward to appreciate the amount of time involved: Ten thousand years ago humans had just discovered agriculture. Writing wouldn't be invented for another 5000 years. Can we really plan 10,000 years into the future? Of course we can't. We have no idea what the world will be like then. There is no way we can claim that we will be able to store nuclear waste for 10,000 years. Any plan to do that is clearly unacceptable.

Of course, calling storage unacceptable is itself an unacceptable answer. We have the waste, and we have to do something with it. But the problem isn't really as hard as I just portrayed it. We don't need absolute security for 10,000 years. A more reasonable goal is to reduce the risk of leakage to 0.1%—that is, to one chance in a thousand. Because the radioactivity is only 1000 times worse than that of the uranium we removed from the ground, the net risk (probability multiplied by danger) is $1000 \times 0.001 = 1$—that is, basically the same as the risk if we hadn't mined the uranium in the first place. (I am assuming the linear hypothesis— that total cancer risk is independent of individual doses or dose rate—but my argument won't depend strongly on its validity.)

Moreover, we don't need this 0.1% level of security for the full 10,000 years. After 300 years, the fission fragment radioactivity will have decreased by a factor of 10; it will be only 100 times as great as the mined uranium. So by then, we no longer need the risk to be at the 0.1% level, but could allow a 1% chance that all of the waste leaks out. That's a lot easier than guaranteeing absolute containment for 10,000 years. Moreover, this calculation assumes that 100% of the waste escapes. For leakage of 1% of the waste, we can accept a 100% probability after 300 years. When you think about it this way, the storage problem begins to seem tractable.

However, the public discussion doesn't take into account these numbers, or the fact that the initial mining actually removed radioactivity from the ground. Instead, the public insists on absolute security. The Department of Energy continues to search Yucca Mountain for unknown earthquake faults, and many people assume that the acceptability of the facility depends on the absence of any such faults. They believe that the discovery of a new fault will rule Yucca Mountain out. The issue, though, should not be whether there will be any earthquakes in the next 10,000 years, but whether after 300 years there will be a 1% chance of a sufficiently large earthquake that 100% of the waste will escape its glass capsules and reach groundwater. Or, we could accept a 100% chance that 1% of the waste will leak, or a 10% chance that 10% will leak. Any of these options leads to a lower risk than if the original uranium had been left in the ground, mixing its natural radioactivity with groundwater. Absolute security is an unnecessarily extreme goal, since even the original uranium in the ground didn't provide it.

The problem is even easier to solve when we ask why we are comparing the danger of waste storage only to the danger of the uranium originally mined. Why not compare it to the larger danger of the natural uranium left in the soil? Colorado, where much of the uranium is obtained, is a geologically active region, full of faults and fissures and mountains rising out of the prairie, and its surface rock contains about a billion tons of uranium. The radioactivity in this uranium is 20 times greater than the legal limit for Yucca Mountain, and it will take more than 13 billion years—not just a few hundred—for the radioactivity to drop by a factor of 10. Yet water that runs through, around, and over this radioactive rock is the source of the Colorado River, which is used for drinking water in much of the West, including Los Angeles and San Diego. And unlike the glass pellets that store the waste in Yucca Mountain, most of the uranium in the Colorado ground is water-soluble. Here is the absurd-sounding conclusion: if the Yucca Mountain facility were at full capacity and all the waste leaked out of its glass containment immediately and managed to reach groundwater, the danger would still be 20 times less than that currently posed by natural uranium leaching into the Colorado River. The situation brings to mind the resident near Three Mile Island who feared the tiny leakage from the reactor but not the much greater radioactivity of natural radon gas seeping up from the ground.

I don't mean to imply that waste from Yucca Mountain is not dangerous. Nor am I suggesting that we should panic about radioactivity in the Los Angeles water supply. The Colorado River example illustrates only that when we worry about mysterious and unfamiliar dangers, we sometimes lose perspective. Every way I do the calculation, I reach the same conclusion: waste leakage from Yucca Mountain is not a great danger. Put the waste in glass pellets in a reasonably stable geologic formation, and start worrying about real threats—such as the dangers of the continued burning of fossil fuels.

A related issue is the risk of mishaps and attacks during the transportation of nuclear waste to the Yucca Mountain site. The present plans call for the waste to be carried in thick, reinforced concrete cylinders that can survive high-speed crashes without leaking. In fact, it would be very hard for a terrorist to open the containers, or to use the waste in radiological weapons. The smart terrorist is more likely to hijack a tanker truck full of gasoline, chlorine, or another common toxic material and then blow it up in a city. Recall from the chapter on terrorist nukes that al-Qaeda told José Padilla to abandon his effort to make a dirty bomb and instead focus his efforts on natural-gas explosions in apartment buildings.

Why are we worrying about transporting nuclear waste? Ironically, we have gone to such lengths to ensure the safety of the transport that the public thinks the danger is greater than it really is. Images on evening newscasts of concrete containers being dropped from five-story buildings, smashing into the ground and bouncing undamaged, do not reassure the public. This is a consequence of the "where there's smoke there's fire" paradox of public safety. Raise the standards, increase the safety, do more research, study the problem in greater depth, and in the process you will improve safety and frighten the public. After all, would scientists work so hard if the threat weren't real? Scientists who propose rocketing the waste to the sun, or burying it in a subduction zone in the ocean, also seem to be suggesting that the problem is truly intractable, and that premise exacerbates the public fear.

See Chapter 7 for tips on saying why it matters.

Agonism in the Academy:
Surviving the Argument Culture

DEBORAH TANNEN

—⊡—

A READING GROUP that I belong to, composed of professors, recently discussed a memoir by an academic. I came to the group's meeting full of anticipation, eager to examine the insights I'd gained from the book and to be enlightened by those that had intrigued my fellow group members. As the meeting began, one member announced that she hadn't read the book; four, including me, said they'd read and enjoyed it; and one said she hadn't liked it because she does not like academic memoirs. She energetically criticized the book. "It's written in two voices," she said, "and the voices don't interrogate each other."

DEBORAH TANNEN is a linguistics professor at Georgetown University and has written widely about how language affects relationships. Her books include *You Just Don't Understand: Women and Men in Conversation* (1990), *The Argument Culture* (1998), *You're Wearing THAT?: Understanding Mothers and Daughters in Conversation* (2006), and *You Were Always Mom's Favorite!: Sisters in Conversation Throughout Their Lives* (2009). This essay was first published in March 2000 in *The Chronicle of Higher Education*.

Quickly, two other members joined her critique, their point of view becoming a chorus. They sounded smarter, seeing faults that the rest of us had missed, making us look naïve. We credulous three tried in vain to get the group talking about what we had found interesting or important in the book, but our suggestions were dull compared to the game of critique.

I left the meeting disappointed because I had learned nothing new about the book or its subject. All I had learned about was the acumen of the critics. I was especially struck by the fact that one of the most talkative and influential critics was the member who had not read the book. Her unfamiliarity with the work had not hindered her, because the critics had focused more on what they saw as faults of the genre than on faults of the particular book.

The turn that the discussion had taken reminded me of the subject of my most recent book, *The Argument Culture*. The phenomenon I'd observed at the book-group meeting was an example of what the cultural linguist Walter Ong calls "agonism," which he defines in *Fighting for Life* as "programmed contentiousness" or "ceremonial combat." Agonism does not refer to disagreement, conflict, or vigorous dispute. It refers to *ritualized* opposition—for instance, a debate in which the contestants are assigned opposing positions and one party wins, rather than an argument that arises naturally when two parties disagree.

See p. 22 for more on beginning with an anecdote to show the view you're challenging.

In *The Argument Culture*, I explored the role and effects of agonism in three domains of public discourse: journalism, politics, and the law. But the domain in which I first identified the phenomenon and began thinking about it is the academic world. I remain convinced that agonism is endemic in academe—and bad for it.

The way we train our students, conduct our classes and our research, and exchange ideas at meetings and in print are all driven by our ideological assumption that intellectual inquiry is a metaphorical battle. Following from that is a second assumption, that the best way to demonstrate intellectual prowess is to criticize, find fault, and attack.

Many aspects of our academic lives can be described as agonistic. For example, in our scholarly papers, most of us follow a conventional framework that requires us to position our work in opposition to someone else's, which we prove wrong. The framework tempts—almost requires—us to oversimplify or even misrepresent others' positions; cite the weakest example to make a generally reasonable work appear less so; and ignore facts that support others' views, citing only evidence that supports our own positions.

The way we train our students frequently reflects the battle metaphor as well. We assign scholarly work for them to read, then invite them to tear it apart. That is helpful to an extent, but it often means that they don't learn to do the harder work of integrating ideas, or of considering the work's historical and disciplinary context. Moreover, it fosters in students a stance of arrogance and narrow-mindedness, qualities that do not serve the fundamental goals of education.

In the classroom, if students are engaged in heated debate, we believe that education is taking place. But in a 1993 article in The History Teacher, Patricia Rosof, who teaches at Hunter College High School in New York City, advises us to look more closely at what's really happening. If we do, she says, we will probably find that only a few students are participating; some other students may be paying attention, but many may be turned off. Furthermore, the students who are arguing generally simplify the points they are making or disputing. To win the argument, they ignore complexity and nuance. They refuse to concede a point raised by their opponents, even if they can see that it is valid, because such a concession would weaken their position. Nobody tries to synthesize the various views, because that would look indecisive, or weak.

If the class engages in discussion rather than debate—adding such intellectual activities as exploring ideas, uncovering nuances, comparing and contrasting different interpretations of a work—more students take part, and more of them gain a deeper, and more accurate, understanding of the material. Most important, the students learn a stance of respect and open-minded inquiry.

Academic rewards—good grades and good jobs—typically go to students and scholars who learn to tear down others' work, not to those who learn to build on the work of their colleagues. In *The Argument Culture*, I cited a study in which communications researchers Karen Tracy and Sheryl Baratz examined weekly colloquia attended by faculty members and graduate students at a large university. As the authors reported in a 1993 article in *Communication Monographs*, although most people said the purpose of the colloquia was to "trade ideas" and "learn things," faculty members in fact were judging the students' competence based on their participation in the colloquia. And the professors didn't admire students who asked "a nice little supportive question," as one put it—they valued "tough and challenging questions."

One problem with the agonistic culture of graduate training is that potential scholars who are not comfortable with that kind of interaction are likely to drop out. As a result, many talented and creative minds are lost to academe. And, with fewer colleagues who prefer different approaches, those who remain are more likely to egg each other on to even greater adversarial heights. Some scholars who do stay in academe are reluctant to present their work at conferences or submit it for publication because of their reluctance to take part in adversarial discourse. The cumulative effect is that nearly everyone feels vulnerable and defensive, and thus less willing to suggest new ideas, offer new perspectives, or question received wisdom.

Although scholarly attacks are ritual—prescribed by the conventions of academe—the emotions propelling them can be real. Jane Tompkins, a literary critic who has written about the genre of the western in modern fiction and film, has compared scholarly exchanges to shootouts. In a 1988 article in *The Georgia Review*, she noted that her own career took off when she published an essay that "began with a frontal assault on another woman scholar. When I wrote it I felt the way the hero does in a western. Not only had this critic argued *a*, *b*, and *c*, she had held *x*, *y*, and *z*! It was a clear case of outrageous provocation." Because her opponent was established and she was not, Tompkins felt "justified in hitting her with everything I had."

Later in her career, as she listened to a speaker at a conference demolish another scholar's work, she felt that she was witnessing "a ritual execution of some sort, something halfway between a bullfight, where the crowd admires the skill of the matador and enjoys his triumph over the bull, and a public burning, where the crowd witnesses the just punishment of a criminal. For the academic experience combined the elements of admiration, bloodlust, and moral self-congratulation."

At a deeper level, the conceptual metaphor of intellectual argument as a battle leads us to divide researchers into warring camps. Just about any field can provide examples. For instance, many disciplines are affected—and disfigured—by a stubborn nature/nurture dichotomy, although both biology and culture obviously influence all of us. Such divisiveness encourages both students and scholars to fight about others' work rather than trying to understand it. And those whose work is misrepresented end up using creative energy to defend their past work—energy that they could use more productively in other ways.

Agonism has still another serious effect: It is one of the reasons scholars have a hard time getting policymakers to pay attention to their research. Policymakers who come across relevant academic research immediately encounter opposing research. Lacking the expertise to figure out who's right, they typically conclude that they cannot look to academe for guidance.

Our agonist ideology seems so deeply embedded in academe that one might wonder what alternatives we have. In *Embracing Contraries*, the English professor Peter Elbow calls the ways we approach ideas a "doubting game"—a method for sniffing out faults. What we need, he says, is an additional approach—a "believing game," to sniff out strengths. The two games would complement each other. Although we wouldn't end up agreeing with all the authors we read, by suspending disbelief we would be more likely to learn something from them.

In my view, we need new metaphors through which to think about our academic enterprise, or to conceptualize intellectual interchange. We could learn much more if we thought of theories not as static structures to be shot down or falsified, but as sets of understandings to be questioned and reshaped. The sociologist Kerry Daly, in the introduction to his book *Families and Time*, suggests that "theories should be treated like bread dough that rises with a synergetic mix of ingredients only to be pounded down with the addition of new ingredients and human energy."

In the realm of teaching, Don McCormick and Michael Kahn, in a 1982 article in *Exchange: The Organizational Behavior Teaching Journal*, suggest that critical thinking can be taught better if we use the metaphor of a barn raising, instead of that of a boxing match. We should think of "a group of builders constructing a building, or a group of artists fabricating a creation together."

McCormick and Kahn make another point that, as I wrote in *The Argument Culture*, I came to believe is the most crucial and damaging aspect of the culture of agonism. Living, working, and thinking in ways shaped by the battle metaphor produces an atmosphere of animosity that poisons our relations with each other at the same time that it corrupts the integrity of our research. Not only is the agonistic culture of academe not the best path to truth and knowledge, but it also is corrosive to the human spirit.

After my reading group had discussed the academic memoir, I expressed my frustration to a group member. She commented, "It turns out that book wasn't the best example of the genre."

"But we didn't read an example of a genre," I protested. "We read a book by a person."

Refocusing our attention in that way is the greatest gain in store if we can move beyond critique in its narrow sense. We would learn more from each other, be heard more clearly by others, attract more varied talents to the scholarly life, and restore a measure of humanity to ourselves, our endeavor, and the academic world we inhabit.

INDEX OF TEMPLATES

—◻—

INTRODUCING WHAT "THEY SAY" *(p. 23)*

- A number of _____ have recently suggested that _____.

- It has become common today to dismiss _____.

- In their recent work, Y and Z have offered harsh critiques of _____ for _____.

INTRODUCING "STANDARD VIEWS"
(pp. 23–24, 162–63, 181–82)

- Americans today tend to believe that _____.

- Conventional wisdom has it that _____.

- Common sense seems to dictate that _____.

- The standard way of thinking about topic X has it that _____.

- It is often said that _____.

- My whole life I have heard it said that _____.

- You would think that _____.

- Many people assume that _____.

MAKING WHAT "THEY SAY"
SOMETHING YOU SAY *(pp. 24–25)*

▸ I've always believed that _____ .

▸ When I was a child, I used to think that _____ .

▸ Although I should know better by now, I cannot help thinking that
_____ .

▸ At the same time that I believe _____ , I also believe _____ .

INTRODUCING SOMETHING
IMPLIED OR ASSUMED *(p. 25)*

▸ Although none of them have ever said so directly, my teachers have
often given me the impression that _____ .

▸ One implication of X's treatment of _____ is that
_____ .

▸ Although X does not say so directly, she apparently assumes that
_____ .

▸ While they rarely admit as much, _____ often take for granted
that _____ .

INTRODUCING AN ONGOING DEBATE
(pp. 25–26, 182–83, 188)

▸ In discussions of X, one controversial issue has been _____ .
On the one hand, _____ argues _____ . On the other hand,
_____ contends _____ . Others even maintain _____ .
My own view is _____ .

Index of Templates

- ▶ When it comes to the topic of _____ , most of us will readily agree that _____ . Where this agreement usually ends, however, is on the question of _____ . Whereas some are convinced that _____ , others maintain that _____ .

- ▶ In conclusion, then, as I suggested earlier, defenders of _____ can't have it both ways. Their assertion that _____ is contradicted by their claim that _____ .

CAPTURING AUTHORIAL ACTION (pp. 38–40)

- ▶ X acknowledges that _____ .

- ▶ X agrees that _____ .

- ▶ X argues that _____ .

- ▶ X believes that _____ .

- ▶ X denies/does not deny that _____ .

- ▶ X claims that _____ .

- ▶ X complains that _____ .

- ▶ X concedes that _____ .

- ▶ X demonstrates that _____ .

- ▶ X deplores the tendency to _____ .

- ▶ X celebrates the fact that _____ .

- ▶ X emphasizes that _____ .

▸ X insists that _____.

▸ X observes that _____.

▸ X questions whether _____.

▸ X refutes the claim that _____.

▸ X reminds us that _____.

▸ X reports that _____.

▸ X suggests that _____.

▸ X urges us to _____.

INTRODUCING QUOTATIONS *(p. 46)*

▸ X states, "_____."

▸ As the prominent philosopher X puts it, "_____."

▸ According to X, "_____."

▸ X himself writes, "_____."

▸ In her book, _____, X maintains that "_____"

▸ Writing in the journal *Commentary*, X complains that "_____."

▸ In X's view, "_____."

▸ X agrees when she writes, "_____."

▸ X disagrees when he writes, "_____."

▸ X complicates matters further when he writes, "_____."

Index of Templates

EXPLAINING QUOTATIONS *(pp. 46–47)*

▸ Basically, X is saying _____ .

▸ In other words, X believes _____ .

▸ In making this comment, X urges us to _____ .

▸ X is corroborating the age-old adage that _____ .

▸ X's point is that _____ .

▸ The essence of X's argument is that _____ .

DISAGREEING, WITH REASONS *(pp. 60, 172–73)*

▸ I think X is mistaken because she overlooks _____ .

▸ X's claim that _____ rests upon the questionable assumption that _____ .

▸ I disagree with X's view that _____ because, as recent research has shown, _____ .

▸ X contradicts herself/can't have it both ways. On the one hand, she argues _____ . On the other hand, she also says _____ .

▸ By focusing on _____ , X overlooks the deeper problem of _____ .

AGREEING—WITH A DIFFERENCE *(pp. 62–64, 170)*

▶ I agree that _____ because my experience _____ confirms it.

▶ X surely is right about _____ because, as she may not be aware, recent studies have shown that _____.

▶ X's theory of _____ is extremely useful because it sheds insight on the difficult problem of _____.

▶ Those unfamiliar with this school of thought may be interested to know that it basically boils down to _____.

▶ I agree that _____, a point that needs emphasizing since so many people believe _____.

▶ If group X is right that _____, as I think they are, then we need to reassess the popular assumption that _____.

AGREEING AND DISAGREEING
SIMULTANEOUSLY *(pp. 64–66, 173–74, 183)*

▶ Although I agree with X up to a point, I cannot accept his overall conclusion that _____.

▶ Although I disagree with much that X says, I fully endorse his final conclusion that _____.

▶ Though I concede that _____, I still insist that _____.

▶ Whereas X provides ample evidence that _____, Y and Z's research on _____ and _____ convinces me that _____ instead.

Index of Templates

- X is right that _____, but she seems on more dubious ground when she claims that _____.

- While X is probably wrong when she claims that _____, she is right that _____.

- I'm of two minds about X's claim that _____. On the one hand, I agree that _____. On the other hand, I'm not sure if _____.

- My feelings on the issue are mixed. I do support X's position that _____, but I find Y's argument about _____ and Z's research on _____ to be equally persuasive.

SIGNALING WHO IS SAYING WHAT *(pp. 71–73)*

- X argues _____.

- According to both X and Y, _____.

- Politicians _____, X argues, should _____.

- Most athletes will tell you that _____.

- My own view, however, is that _____.

- I agree, as X may not realize, that _____.

- But _____ are real and, arguably, the most significant factor in _____.

- But X is wrong that _____.

- However, it is simply not true that _____.

- Indeed, it is highly likely that _____.

▸ X's assertion that _____ does not fit the facts.

▸ X is right that _____.

▸ X is wrong that _____.

▸ X is both right and wrong that _____.

▸ Yet a sober analysis of the matter reveals _____.

▸ Nevertheless, new research shows _____.

▸ Anyone familiar with _____ should agree that _____.

EMBEDDING VOICE MARKERS *(pp. 74–75)*

▸ X overlooks what I consider an important point about _____.

▸ My own view is that what X insists is a _____ is in fact a _____.

▸ I wholeheartedly endorse what X calls _____.

▸ These conclusions, which X discusses in _____, add weight to the argument that _____.

ENTERTAINING OBJECTIONS *(pp. 82, 174–75, 193–94)*

▸ At this point I would like to raise some objections that have been inspired by the skeptic in me. She feels that I have been ignoring _____. " _____," she says to me, " _____."

▸ Yet some readers may challenge the view that _____.

▸ Of course, many will probably disagree with this assertion that _____.

Index of Templates

NAMING YOUR NAYSAYERS *(pp. 83–84)*

▸ Here many *feminists* would probably object that ＿＿＿＿.

▸ But *social Darwinists* would certainly take issue with the argument that ＿＿＿＿.

▸ *Biologists,* of course, may want to question whether ＿＿＿＿.

▸ Nevertheless, both *followers and critics of Malcom X* will probably argue that ＿＿＿＿.

▸ Although not all *Christians* think alike, some of them will probably dispute my claim that ＿＿＿＿.

▸ *Non-native English speakers* are so diverse in their views that it's hard to generalize about them, but some are likely to object on the grounds that ＿＿＿＿.

INTRODUCING OBJECTIONS INFORMALLY *(pp. 84–85)*

▸ But is my proposal realistic? What are the chances of its actually being adopted?

▸ Yet is it always true that ＿＿＿＿? Is it always the case, as I have been suggesting, that ＿＿＿＿?

▸ However, does the evidence I've cited prove conclusively that ＿＿＿＿?

▸ "Impossible," some will say. "You must be reading the research selectively."

MAKING CONCESSIONS WHILE STILL STANDING YOUR GROUND *(pp. 89)*

▶ Although I grant that _____, I still maintain that _____.

▶ Proponents of X are right to argue that _____. But they exaggerate when they claim that _____.

▶ While it is true that _____, it does not necessarily follow that _____.

▶ On the one hand, I agree with X that _____. But on the other hand, I still insist that _____.

INDICATING WHO CARES *(pp. 95–96)*

▶ _____ used to think _____. But recently [or within the past few decades] _____ suggests that _____.

▶ These findings challenge the work of earlier researchers, who tended to assume that _____.

▶ Recent studies like these shed new light on _____, which previous studies had not addressed.

▶ Researchers have long assumed that _____. For instance, one eminent scholar of cell biology, _____, assumed in _____, her seminal work on cell structures and functions, that fat cells _____. As _____ herself put it, "_____" (2007). Another leading scientist, _____, argued that fat cells "_____" (2006). Ultimately, when it came to the nature of fat, the basic assumption was that _____.

But a new body of research shows that fat cells are far more complex and that _____.

▸ If sports enthusiasts stopped to think about it, many of them might simply assume that the most successful athletes _____. However, new research shows _____.

▸ These findings challenge neoliberals' common assumptions that _____.

▸ At first glance, teenagers appear to _____. But on closer inspection _____.

ESTABLISHING WHY YOUR CLAIMS MATTER
(pp. 98–99, 175–76, 194–96)

▸ X matters/is important because _____.

▸ Although X may seem trivial, it is in fact crucial in terms of today's concern over _____.

▸ Ultimately, what is at stake here is _____.

▸ These findings have important consequences for the broader domain of _____.

▸ My discussion of X is in fact addressing the larger matter of _____.

▸ These conclusions/This discovery will have significant applications in _____ as well as in _____.

▸ Although X may seem of concern to only a small group of _____, it should in fact concern anyone who cares about _____.

COMMONLY USED TRANSITIONS

CAUSE AND EFFECT

accordingly

as a result

consequently

hence

it follows, then

since

so

then

therefore

thus

CONCLUSION

as a result

consequently

hence

in conclusion, then

in short

in sum, then

it follows, then

so

the upshot of all this is that

therefore

thus

to sum up

to summarize

COMPARISON

along the same lines

in the same way

likewise

similarly

CONTRAST

although

but

by contrast

conversely

despite

even though

nevertheless

nonetheless

on the contrary

on the other hand

regardless

whereas

Adding Metacommentary *(pp. 135–37)*

▸ In other words, _____.

▸ What _____ really means by this is _____.

▸ Ultimately, my goal is to demonstrate that _____.

▸ My point is not _____, but _____.

▸ To put it another way, _____.

▸ In sum, then, _____.

▸ My conclusion, then, is that, _____.

▸ In short, _____.

▸ What is more important, _____.

▸ Incidentally, _____.

▸ By the way, _____.

▸ Chapter 2 explores _____, while Chapter 3 examines _____.

▸ Having just argued that _____, let us now turn our attention to _____.

▸ Although some readers may object that _____, I would answer that _____.

Comparing Two or More Studies' Findings
(p. 168)

▸ Our data *support/confirm/verify* the work of X by showing that _____.

▸ By demonstrating _____, X's work *extends* the findings of Y.

▸ The results of X *contradict/refute* Y's conclusion that _____.

▸ X's findings *call into question* the widely accepted theory that _____.

▸ Our data *are consistent with* X's hypothesis that _____.

EXPLAINING AN EXPERIMENTAL RESULT
(pp. 171, 193)

▸ One explanation for X's finding of _____ is that _____. An alternative explanation is _____.

▸ The difference between _____ and _____ is probably due to _____.

INTRODUCING GAPS IN THE EXISTING RESEARCH
(p. 184)

▸ Studies of X have indicated _____. It is not clear, however, that this conclusion applies to _____.

▸ _____ often take for granted that _____. Few have investigated this assumption, however.

▸ X's work tells us a great deal about _____. Can this work be generalized to _____?

ACKNOWLEDGMENTS

—◻—

We have our superb editor, Marilyn Moller, to thank for this book. It was Marilyn who first encouraged us to write it, and she has devoted herself tirelessly to helping us at every stage of the process. We never failed to benefit from her incisive suggestions, her unfailing patience, and her cheerful good humor. With the publication of this second edition, coming on the heels of a trade edition and a version with readings, our debt to Marilyn has greatly multiplied.

Our thanks go as well to John Darger, Norton's Chicago representative, who also offered early encouragement to write *"They Say/I Say,"* and to Beth Ammerman, who generously managed the editing of this edition. Thanks too go to Maggie Wagner, for the striking design; to Jane Searle, for her superb management of the production process; to Debra Morton Hoyt, for her excellent work on the cover; and to Ana Cooke and Betsye Mullaney, for helping with many things large and small.

We owe a special debt of gratitude to Christopher Gillen and Erin Ackerman for their chapters on writing in the hard and social sciences, respectively, that are new to this edition. Working with Chris and Erin proved to be an exhilarating experience. At the same time as they remained open and receptive to our suggestions, they taught us a great deal by applying our ideas to their disciplines in ways that were a constant revelation.

We owe special thanks to our colleagues in the English department at the University of Illinois at Chicago: Mark Canuel, our current department head, for supporting our efforts overseeing the university's Writing in the Disciplines requirement, work that led us to solicit the two new chapters on writing in the sciences and social sciences for this edition. Walter Benn Michaels, our former department head, and Ann Feldman, Director of University Writing Programs, for encouraging us to teach first-year composition courses at UIC in which we could try out ideas and drafts of our manuscript. Lon Kaufman, Tom Moss, Diane Chin, Vainis Aleksa, and Matt Pavesich have also been very supportive of our efforts. We are especially grateful to Ann and Diane for bringing us into their graduate course on the teaching of writing, and to Ann, Tom, Diane, and Matt for inviting us to present our ideas in UIC's Mile 8 workshops for writing instructors. The encouragement, suggestions, and criticisms we received at these sessions have proved invaluable. Our deep gratitude also goes to our research assistant for the past two years, Matt Oakes.

We are also especially grateful to Steve Benton and Nadya Pittendrigh, who taught a section of composition with us using an early draft of this book. Steve made many helpful suggestions, particularly regarding the exercises. We are grateful to Andy Young, a lecturer at UIC who has tested our book in his courses and who gave us extremely helpful feedback. And we thank Vershawn A. Young, whose work on code-meshing influenced our argument in Chapter 9, and Hillel Crandus, whose classroom handout inspired Chapter 11, "Entering Classroom Discussions."

We are grateful to the many colleagues and friends who've let us talk our ideas out with them and given extremely helpful responses. UIC's former dean, Stanley Fish, has been central in this respect, both in personal conversations and in his incisive articles calling for greater focus on form in the teaching of writing. Our conversations with Jane Tompkins have also been integral to this book, as was the composition course that Jane co-taught with Gerald entitled "Can We Talk?" Lenny Davis, too, offered both intellectual insight and emotional support, as did Heather Arnet, Jennifer Ashton, Janet Atwill, Kyra Auslander, Noel Barker, Jim Benton, Jack Brereton, Tim Cantrick, Marsha Cassidy, David Chinitz, Lisa Chinitz, Pat Chu, Duane Davis, Bridget O'Rourke Flisk, Steve Flisk, Judy Gardiner, Howard Gardner, Rich Gelb, Gwynne Gertz, Jeff Gore, Bill Haddad, Ben Hale, Scott Hammerl, Patricia Harkin, Andy Hoberek, John Huntington, Joe Janangelo, Paul Jay, David Jolliffe, Nancy Kohn, Don Lazere, Jo Liebermann, Steven Mailloux, Deirdre McCloskey, Maurice J. Meilleur, Allan Meyers, Greg Meyerson, Alan Meyers, Anna Minkov, Chris Newfield, Jim Phelan, Paul Psilos, Bruce Robbins, Charles Ross, Evan Seymour, Eileen Seifert, David Shumway, Herb Simons, Jim Sosnoski, David Steiner, Harold Veeser, Chuck Venegoni, Marla Weeg, Jerry Wexler, Joyce Wexler, Virginia Wexman, Jeffrey Williams, Lynn Woodbury, and the late Wayne Booth, whose friendship we dearly miss.

We are grateful for having had the opportunity to present our ideas to a number of schools: Augustana College, Brandeis University, Brigham Young University, Bryn Mawr College, Case Western University, Columbia University, Community College of Philadelphia, California State University at Bakersfield, California State University at Northridge, University of California at Riverside, University of Delaware, DePauw University, Drew University, Duke University, Duquesne University, Elmhurst College, Fontbonne University, Furman University, Gettysburg College, Harper College, Harvard University, Haverford College, Hunter College, Illinois State University, John Carroll University, Lawrence University, the Lawrenceville School, MacEwan University, University of Maryland at College Park, University of Memphis, University of Missouri at Columbia, New Trier High School, Northern Michigan University, North Carolina A&T University, State University of New York at Stony Brook, University of North Florida, Northwestern University Division of Continuing Studies, University of Notre Dame, Oregon State University, University of Portland, University of Rochester, St. Ambrose University, St. Andrew's School, St. Charles High School, Seattle University, Southern Connecticut State University, University of South Florida, Swarthmore College, Teachers College, University of Tennessee at Knoxville, University of Texas at Arlington, Tulane University, Union College, Wabash College, Washington College, University of Washington, Western Michigan University, University of West Virginia at Morgantown, Whitney Young High School, and the University of Wisconsin at Whitewater.

We particularly thank those who helped arrange these visits and discussed writing issues with us: Jeff Abernathy, Herman Asarnow, John Austin, Greg Barnheisel, John Bean, Crystal Benedicks, Joe Bizup, Sheridan Blau, Dagne Bloland, Chris Breu, Joan Johnson Bube, John Caldwell, Gregory Clark, Irene Clark, Dean Philip Cohen, Cathy D'Agostino, Tom Deans, Gaurav Desai, Kathleen Dudden-Rowlands, Lisa Ede, Emory Elliott, Anthony Ellis, Kim Flachmann, Ronald Fortune, George Haggerty, Donald Hall, Gary Hatch, Elizabeth Hatmaker, Harry Hellenbrand, Nicole Henderson, Doug Hesse, Joe

Harris, Van Hillard, Andrew Hoberek, Michael Hustedde, Sara Jameson, T. R. Johnson, David Jones, Ann Kaplan, Don Kartiganer, Linda Kinnahan, Dean Georg Kleine, Albert Labriola, Tom Liam Lynch, Thomas McFadden, Sean Meehan, Connie Mick, Margaret Oakes, John O'Connor, Gary Olson, Tom Pace, Emily Poe, Dominick Randolph, Monica Rico, Kelly Ritter, Jack Robinson, Warren Rosenberg, Dean Howard Ross, Deborah Rossen-Knill, Rose Shapiro, Mike Shea, Evan Seymour, Erec Smith, Nancy Sommers, Stephen Spector, Timothy Spurgin, Ron Strickland, Trig Thoreson, Josh Toth, Judy Trost, Charles Tung, John Webster, Sandi Weisenberg, Robert Weisbuch, Martha Woodmansee, and Lynn Worsham.

For inviting us to present our ideas at their conferences, we are grateful to John Brereton and Richard Wendorf at the Boston Athenaeum; Wendy Katkin of the Reinvention Center of SUNY Stony Brook; Luchen Li of the Michigan English Association; Lisa Lee and Barbara Ransby of the Public Square in Chicago; Don Lazere of the University of Tennessee at Knoxville, chair of a panel at the MLA; Dennis Baron of the University of Illinois at Urbana-Champaign, Alfie Guy of Yale University, Gregory Colomb of the University of Virginia, and Irene Clark of the California State University of Northridge, chairs of panels at CCCC; George Crandell and Steve Hubbard, co-directors of the ACETA conference at Auburn University; Mary Beth Rose of the Humanities Institute at the University of Illinois at Chicago; Diana Smith of St. Anne's Belfield School and the University of Virginia; Jim Maddox and Victor Luftig of the Bread Loaf School of English; Jan Fitzsimmons and Jerry Berberet of the Associated Colleges of Illinois; and Rosemary Feal, Executive Director of the Modern Language Association, initiator of a workshop for community college teachers at the 2008 MLA convention.

A very special thanks goes to those who reviewed the materials for this new edition: Erin Ackerman (City University of New York–John Jay College); Mary Angeline (University of Northern Colorado); Ned Bachus; Michelle Ballif (University of Georgia); Jonathan Barz (University of Dubuque); Mary Bauer Morley (University of North Dakota); Benjamin Bennett-Carpenter (Oakland University); Michelle Boswell (University of Maryland); Laura Bowles (University of Central Arkansas); E Brand (Broome Community College); Beth Buyserie (Washington State University); Dana Cairns Watson (University of California, Los Angeles); Genevieve Carminati (Montgomery College); Brent Chesley (Aquinas College); Joseph Colavito (Butler University); Tara DaPra (University of Minnesota); Emily Detmer-Goebel (Northern Kentucky University); J. Michael Duvall (College of Charleston); Adriana Estill (Carleton College); Ralph Faris (Community College of Philadelphia); Chris Gillen (Kenyon College); Patricia Gillikin (University of New Mexico Valencia Campus); Kenneth Grant (University of Wisconsin–Baraboo/Sauk County); Kevin Griffith (Capital University); Annemarie Hamlin (Central Oregon Community College); Rick Hansen (California State University, Fresno); John Hare (Montgomery College); Wendy Hayden (Hunter College of the City University of New York); Karen Head (Georgia Institute of Technology); Chene Heady (Longwood University); Nels Highberg (University of Hartford); Victoria Holladay (California State University, Los Angeles); D. Kern Holoman (University of California, Davis); Elizabeth Huergo (Montgomery College); Sara Jameson (Oregon State University); Joseph Jones (University of Memphis); Andrew

Keitt (University of Alabama at Birmingham); Kurt Koenigs-berger (Case Western Reserve University); Gary Leising (Utica College); Gary Lewandowski (Monmouth University); Michelle Maher (La Roche College); Lisa Martin (University of Wisconsin–Baraboo/Sauk County); Miles McCrimmon (J. Sargeant Reynolds Community College); Jacqueline Megow (Oklahoma State University); Bruce Michelson (University of Illinois–Urbana Champaign); Megan Morton (Purdue University); Steven Muhlberger (Nipissing University); Lori Muntz (Iowa Wesleyan College); Ann Murphy (Assumption College); Sarah Perrault (University of Nevada, Reno); Christine Pipitone-Herron (Raritan Valley Community College); David Samper (University of Oklahoma); Rose Shapiro (Fontbonne University); Jennifer Stewart (Indiana University–Purdue University Fort Wayne); Sandra Stollman (Broward College); Linda Sturtz (Beloit College); Mark Sutton (Kean University); Tobin von der Nuell (University of Colorado at Boulder); Brody Waybrant (Bay Mills Community College); Gina Weaver (Southern Nazarene University); Amy Whitson (Missouri State University); Susan Wright (Montclair State University).

Thanks also goes to those who reviewed the manuscript for the original version of "They Say"; their suggestions contributed enormously to this book: Alan Ainsworth (Houston Community College); Rise Axelrod (University of California, Riverside); Bob Baron (Mesa Community College); David Bartholomae (University of Pittsburgh); Diane Belcher (Georgia State University); Michel De Benedictis (Miami Dade College); Joseph Bizup (Columbia University); Patricia Bizzell (College of the Holy Cross); John Brereton (Harvard University); Richard Bullock (Wright State University); Charles Cooper (University of California, San Diego); Christine Cozzens (Agnes Scott College); Sarah Duerden (Arizona State University); Russel Durst

(University of Cincinnati); Joseph Harris (Duke University); Paul Heilker (Virginia Polytechnic Institute); Michael Hennessy (Texas State University); Karen Lunsford (University of California, Santa Barbara); Libby Miles (University of Rhode Island); Mike Rose (University of California, Los Angeles); William H. Smith (Weatherford College); Scott Stevens (Western Washington University); Patricia Sullivan (University of Colorado); Pamela Wright (University of California, San Diego); Daniel Zimmerman (Middlesex Community College).

GERALD GRAFF, a professor of English and Education at the University of Illinois at Chicago and 2008 President of the Modern Language Association of America, has had a major impact on teachers through such books as *Professing Literature: An Institutional History*, *Beyond the Culture Wars: How Teaching the Conflicts Can Revitalize American Education*, and, most recently, *Clueless in Academe: How Schooling Obscures the Life of the Mind*. CATHY BIRKENSTEIN is a lecturer in English at the University of Illinois at Chicago and co-director of the Writing in the Disciplines program. She has published essays on writing, most recently in *College English*, and, with Gerald Graff, in *The Chronicle of Higher Education*, *Academe*, and *College Composition and Communication*. She has also given talks and workshops with Gerald at numerous colleges and is currently working on a study of common misunderstandings surrounding academic discourse.

245